LEADERSHIP

.....IN THE WORLD'S GREATEST BUSINESS...

....THE CHURCH

Copyright © 2018 by Benjamin A. Griffin

All rights reserved. No part of this book shall be reproduced or transmitted in any form or by any means, electronic, mechanical without the express permission of the author.

ISBN-13: 978-1982071417
ISBN-10: 1982071419

A product of IFC Ministry and Plumline Leadership, LLC

Printed in the USA

Acknowledgements

A purposeful hope is to encourage Christian leadership and education, by conveying and emphasizing what is required of those who would find themselves leading In the World's Greatest Business - the Church.

"Dr. Griffin has written an excellent fact-based, comprehensive book on leadership. He draws on his substantial personal leadership experience and solid research. Always faithful to the Word, Dr. Griffin has provided a valuable resource for those who aspire to leadership and those who are now bearing the heavy responsibility of leading God's people."- **Jim Benton, Ph.D., President,** The Theological University of America.

"This text presents an excellent and scholarly insight into a situation that warrants the attention of academics worldwide: the plight of scholarly credentials diligently attained through religious academies. It is both well written and pointed in its approach to representing the facts of the issue with objectivity and balance. It is a very profitable read for everyone in the religious and secular realm." - **Ray Gosa Sr.,** Master Teacher, Palm Beach County School System.

"Leadership, In the World's Greatest Business, the Church" is required reading for anyone who is currently or aspires to be a church leader. Effective leadership ability is a requirement to be successful as a Pastor in today's world."- **Dale Smith,** Retired Corporate Executive in Human Resource, and International Philanthropist.

"A powerful message about leadership in today's complex world! A must read for all who care about our future" **Dr. Edwin West, President, The Masonboro Group.**

A special thanks to Plumline Leadership, the originating cause for this book project.

Dedication

This book is dedicated to the Kingdom of Christ, the Wilmington Central and Suncoast churches of Christ in Wilmington, North Carolina and in Lake Worth, Florida respectively, who supported me during the writing of this book. And May God be with you.

To all the men of God who paved the way that I may freely speak concerning the truth of the Gospel, and the seriousness of Leadership in Christ's church.

To my wife, my children, my mother for their support, and all those who encouraged me to write and assisted me in proof-reading my book. I am eternally indebted to you.

And again, Thanks

Table of Content

**The
Purpose
Introduction
Chapters**
1. Leadership and its Importance 12
2. Greatest Business in the World? 18
3. Leading as an Elder, Bishop, Shepherd, Pastor, Overseer 25
4. Leading as a Deacon 32
5. Leading as a Preacher/Evangelist 37
6. Leading as a Teacher 44
7. Leading as a Ministry Leader 51
8. Women in Church Leadership 57
9. Modeling Leadership - Acquiring 63
10. Modeling Leadership – Practice 73
11. Modeling Leadership - Self Leadership 78
12. Modeling Leadership - Team Building 85
13. Modeling Leadership – Organizational 91

**An Open Discussion 99
Conclusion 101
Appendixes 104
About the Author 128
Bibliography / References 130**

Purpose

The motivation for writing this book is first and foremost to glorify God, encourage Christian leadership and education and to advance the cause of Christ. The primary purpose of writing this book is to convey and emphasize what is required of those who would find themselves leading in the world's greatest business - the Church. A companion purpose for writing this book is to demonstrate that the principles of education in Christian leadership are principles that provide secular business with solid leadership outcomes.

Most people are unaware of the challenges and criticism that those who obtain a quality education from Christian colleges and universities face as they make application to secular academic institutions and corporations for employment. Unfortunately, this author has personally been told, "you have an excellent background and your credentials are impeccable. The only thing that will keep you from being hired is the word 'Bible' on your diploma. Otherwise, you would be in".

Often, highly educated and imminently qualified Christian leaders are rejected as emotionally and educationally unprepared to make hard decisions and perhaps will be "too preachy" to lead to company growth or to carry-out and fulfill the mission of secular organizations. Non-church men and women who lead in business often are misled by the presence of a religious title in job applicant's educational resume. Without any understanding of the content of the business and leadership courses completed by the job applicant, the employer assumes that the job applicant is not equipped to conceive, apply and produce positive outcomes.

Therefore, this book will also present the case that Christian leadership education and experience (CLEE) embodies modern leadership theories and is equal to or greater than secular education instruction and experiences.

Introduction

We are living in exciting days of the Lord's church. Across the land, congregations are moving forward by faith as more and more people are becoming involved in the ongoing growth in Christian ministry. Why is this happening? In a word ---"Leadership", this is the key. Men of outstanding abilities are involved in leadership on all levels. This phenomenon has produced a renewed interest in leadership training as the man in the pew has become excited about the work in the church and his role in it. He is no longer content to sit still and let "George do it." As one Elder put it, "We are taking leadership training more seriously than we have ever before." Amen!

Unfortunately, the one enduring issue that continues to curse the church is not a lack of resources, not a lack of strategies, not a lack of programs, but a lack of Leadership. What does it take to lead a church to grow as God intended? It certainly takes more than the desire to grow. Many leaders struggle with motivating and involving members in the midst of busy lifestyles as they find it difficult to concentrate on their key biblical roles and responsibilities with so many peripheral issues demanding their attention. In spite of the challenge to equip the church with solid leaders, we must never forget that "Bad men will, when good men won't". In Judges 9:8-16, we have one of the few parables in the Old Testament. It shows an engagement of selecting a king from among upright men to reign over the people of God in Shechem. Unfortunately because, none of the upright men would sacrifice their comfort zone to lead God's people, by default they allowed an unjust, unrighteous, and unfair man ascend to the kingship. Whenever those who know to do the right thing refuse to, it opens the door for evil. Churches must ensure that they are raising men of integrity, so when the time comes to replace or install new leaders, it will have those who know to take the lead, and not leave the Lord's work in the hands of men of ill will. Leaders with integrity are a rare breed within a group of citizens, whose utmost concern is, "What is in it for me?" A selfish society does not always select a leader for their integrity, but for their ability to manipulate a quick fix for chronic problems. It is short-sightedness that can set back a generation, because of their leader's greed and corruption. However, men of integrity understand the big picture of principled leadership, and they value fear of God, trustworthiness and honest economics. A leader of integrity looks out over the long term and discovers what is best for the church, and families.

It's worthy to note that leaders are essential to the work of the church, and no matter how naturally gifted some might be, are in need of being developed. There is no shortage of opinions as to how we can and must reverse these troubling trends and make healthy, growing churches the rule rather than the exception. Leadership is an inevitable calling and may be acquired through various avenues. You may already be in leadership and do a good job, but good leaders are always striving to become better ones. Leadership appears to be glamorous but is more often lonely and thankless.

    My hope in this book is to strike a chord in the hearts of those who are stimulated with the thought of leading others. As we shall see, the best Leaders are actually Servants. "God wants leaders who will match the mountains of life."

Benjamin A. Griffin, Sr.

Chapter 1
Leadership
"You have got to show up if you want to lead"

What is Leadership?

There have been thousands of books and articles written; workshops, seminars, and retreats conducted to gain a better understanding of this all-encompassing subject. Men are reluctant to accept both brief and lengthy definitions and descriptions given concerning leadership because of their own ideas. I am among those who constantly search for what we think is the paramount meaning and the ultimate way of it, only to find ourselves searching even more. However, there are many serious students on this subject who have attempted to define it. But, defining it can be an elusive thing. Is it a position? Is it a person? Is it a process? Maybe it is power and influence. The confusion over how to define leadership grows out of the complexity of leadership itself. The nature of leadership differs from situation to situation. Let's consider just a few:

A Secular perspective

"A leader is a person with certain qualities of personality and character, which are appropriate to the general situation and supported by a degree of relevant technical knowledge and experience, who is able to provide the necessary functions to guide a group towards the further realization of its purpose, while maintaining and building its unity as a team; doing all this in the right ration or proportion with the contributions of other members of the team." John Adair, Action-Centered Leadership

"Leadership is the process of persuasion or example by which an individual (or leadership team) induces a group to pursue objectives held by a leader or shared by a leader and his or her followers."   John W. Gardner, On Leadership

"Leadership is a process that helps direct and mobilize people and/or ideas. Leadership within a complex organization achieves this function through three sub-processes: establishing direction, aligning people, motivating and inspiring."
      John P. Kotter, a Force of Change

"Leadership is a relationship in which one person seeks to influence the thoughts, behaviors, beliefs or values of another person." Walters C. Wright Jr., Relational Leadership

A Spiritual Perspective

"Leadership is a dynamic process in which a man or women with God-given capacity influences a specific group of God's people toward His purpose for that group." J. Robert Clinton, The Making of a Leader

"Leadership involves a person, group, or organization who shows the way in an area of life - whether in the short or the long term - and in doing so both influences and empowers enough people to bring about change in that area. From a Christian point of view it is only when the direction and the method are in-line with God's purposes, character, and ways of operating that godly leadership takes place." Robert Blake and Bernice M. Ledbetter, Reviewing Leadership

"Spiritual Leadership is moving people onto God's agenda." Henry Blackaby and Richard Blackaby, Spiritual Leadership

"Leadership is influence, the ability of one person to influence others" J. Oswald Sanders, Spiritual Leadership

As you can identify, these definitions differ in ways, and these differences have resulted in various researchers exploring very different aspects of leadership. Even though this multiplicity of definitions seems confusing, it is important to understand that there is no single perfect definition. The various definitions can help us appreciate the multitude of factors that affect leadership, as well as different perspectives from which to view it.

The Importance of Leadership

There are few things more important to human activity than leadership. Effective leadership helps our nation through times of perils. It makes a business organization successful. It enables a not-for-profit organization to fulfill its mission. The effective leadership of parents enables children to grow strong and healthy and become productive adults. Leadership sustains our faith in God. The absence of leadership is equally dramatic in its effects. Without leadership, organizations move slowly, stagnate, and lose their way.

Furthermore, problems of implementation are real issues about how leaders influence behavior, change the course of events, and overcome resistance. Leadership is crucial in implementing decisions successfully. "Each of us recognizes the importance of leadership when we vote for our political leaders. We realize that it matters who is in office, so we participate in a contest, an election, to choose the best candidate. Leadership can be used for good or ill. Sometimes people in business have great leadership skills, but put them to terrible uses" (Mills, 2005).

It is important that a leader be able to express his or her vision clearly and in a compelling manner so that others are engaged by it. It is important that a leader has to make a commitment to his or her vision, to the organization, and to the members of the organization. A leader can't be committed one day and uninterested the next. People will judge a leader by his or her commitment, and will commit themselves no more the leader does (Mills, et al., 2005).

Without leadership, a group of human beings quickly degenerates into argument and conflict, because we see things in different ways and lean toward different solutions. Leadership helps to point us in the same direction and harness our efforts jointly. Leadership is the ability to get people to do something significant that they might not otherwise do. It's energizing people toward a goal. "A mob is indecisive, we must have leadership".

Chapter 1
Questions for Reflection and Discussion

1. In your own words express what's the differences between the secular and spiritual definition of leadership?

2. Describe a time when you had to display an unusual act of leadership.

3. Why is leadership important in your context?

4. Explain the difficulty of implementing leadership principles in a church or organization where leadership training is unpopular.

5. Explain why God holds Christians responsible for becoming leaders.

Chapter 2
Greatest Business in the World, the Church!
"Lead tomorrow by learning today"

Now that leadership has been discussed, its meaning, its importance - let's get to the point of the book, leading in the greatest business in the world. Now, I realize that most of you are thinking, "where he gets off saying such a far-fetched, improbable thing as the Church is the greatest business in the world"? Well, it caused you to read the book right? So, where do we start? As to providing empirical proof, I chose not to do so in this book; even though there is much research literature and data that does so. However, the information that I will share with you in this book, I believe will adequately convince you. As mentioned in the purpose of this book, a portion of it was to make aware the recognition of Church Leadership Education and Experience (CLEE) as an appropriate fit to corporate or secular academic success which is often presented with bias and prejudice that suggest that (CLEE) is not usually considered viable in the marketplace. Therefore, let's began with some marketplace language in order to set the tone for our discussion. Another thing, before I go any farther I want to express my indebtedness to the late Brother Franklin Camp, who in his book 'Principles and Perils of

Leadership" (1984) where I first learned of the concept of the Church as being the greatest business in the world in this context. "The greatest business in the world has to be the most far-reaching, most numerical in terms of employees and more financially stable than any other business in the world, most would agree" (p.46). There is a long-standing debate, even among believers, over whether the church is a business or not. Generally, a business is "an organization established for generating profit; a commercial organization." As such, the church is not a business. It is an organization established by God for the primary purpose of worshiping Him and spreading the good news of salvation to mankind. On the other hand, Jesus came to be about his father's business (Luke 2:49), of which was to seek and save the lost (Luke 19:10); which is done solely through and by the church (Acts 2:47). So then Jesus' church is in the business of saving souls, right? The church was created "to the intent that now the manifold wisdom of God might be made known by the church to the principalities and powers in the heavenly places, according to the eternal purpose which He accomplished in Christ Jesus our Lord"(Ephesians 3:10-11).

Born in the Marketplace

Jesus was in touch with the marketplace from the very beginning of his life on earth. He was born in a place of business, the stable of an Inn

(Luke 2:7). Rather than religious leaders, Jesus' first visitors were employees and small business owners. They were shepherds (Luke 2:15-20). We may easily see Jesus as a teacher by virtue of how well he taught and because in the Gospels Jesus is referred to as a Rabbi. However, picturing him as a businessman is what we have most difficulty doing today. Yet in the Gospels the opposite was true. At first, Jesus was recognizable as a businessman than as a rabbi or a ruler (Silvoso, 2006). Shortly after He began to preach, His neighbors in Nazareth asked, "Is this not the carpenter, the son of Mary" (Mark 6:3). By trade Jesus was a businessman, His neighbors may not have seen him in this light but he was. He was described earlier in (Matthew 13:55) as the "carpenter's son" but later in (Mark 6:3) as the "carpenter", which could indicate that the family business was passed on to him, perhaps if Joseph his father had died. This business provided a living for at least eight family members. Jesus' parables show that he was thoroughly familiar with the marketplace and its operation. He was familiar with:
- Construction, Matthew 7:24-27, Wine-making, Luke 5:37-38, Farming, Mark 4:2-20, Ranching, Matthew 18:12-14, Management and labor, Matthew 20:1-16, Family-owned businesses, Matthew 21:28-31, Hostile takeovers, Luke 20:9-19, Return on investments, Matthew 25:14-30,

Management criteria, Luke 12:16-21, Crop yield, Mark 13:27-32.
- Venture capital in high-risk situations, Luke 19:1-27 (adapted from Ed Silvoso, 2006, Anointed for Business).

Qualities of Greatness

Obviously then, the greatest business in the world calls for dedicated and consecrated leadership. The greater part of the business world is made up of big business. Therefore, the enormity of the business of the Church makes it possible for it to be the greatest business in the world. I want to encourage you to think of it as the biggest business in the world. And I want to point out some things that show the Church as the greatest enterprise on earth. The Church, as the greatest business in the world, has the greatest head, Jesus "And hath put all things under his feet to head over all things to the church, which is his body, the fullness of Him that filleth all in all" (Ephesians 1:22-23, Heb. 4:15; Matt. 20:18-20). Sometimes businesses fail not because they were not good ones, but because of the one leading them (Camp, et al., 1984). The church is the greatest business in the world because it has the greatest product and territory in the world. No enterprise has offered mankind what the church has, that is, a new life - salvation. This new life is not only new, it is an abundantly new life and it is one of a kind, and can be only obtained from one supplier (Acts

4:12; Romans 1:16; John 10:10). There are no businesses in the world that have a territory that equals that of the Church. There are many enterprises in which their territories are limited because of the nature of their products, but this is not true of the Church. There is not a single nation of the earth that is not included in the territory that God gave the Church. The heart of men around the world is the territory of God; (Matt. 28:19; Acts 8:36-38) "If thou believe with all thy heart, they mayest." No business on earth may say that it has a potential customer everywhere in the world, every single accountable person; but the Church can (Camp, et al., 1984).

A Plan for Success

In (Mark 16:15, 16) the Lord Jesus said, "Go ye into the entire world and preach the gospel to every creature." The Church has the greatest potential because it is has a worldwide, and international mission and strategic plan, "for God would have all men to be saved and come to the knowledge of the truth" (1 Tim. 2:3-5; 2 Peter 3:9). It is the greatest business in the world because it has the greatest work and cooperation. Its work is to present every man anew in Christ and to make known the manifold wisdom of God (Ephesians 3:11; Colossians 1:28). Most businesses greatest concern is to increase it's bottom-line and if it means to cut cost and people from its work-force, then so be it. If that means to slow down production or expansion then so be it. The church is always adding, never stops expanding, never shutting down, "be ye steadfast, unmovable always abounding in the work of the Lord, because your labor is not is vain" (1 Corinthians 15:58).

Success is guaranteed because of the great cooperation that exists within the church. The greatest business in the world demands the greatest amount of cooperation. "Then the disciples, every man according to his ability, determined to send relief unto the brethren that dwelt in Judea" (Acts 11:29). "They were of one heart and one soul, and not one of them said that aught of things which he possessed was his own" (4:32). There is none other business in the world or has been in the world that functions like the church. It has the greatest urgency, the greatest motivation, the greatest inspiration, dedication, principles and understanding of humankind and is concentrated on the clearest mission. And since the church is the greatest business in the world, it demands the greatest leaders in the world. The church will continue to produce great elders, deacons, preachers, teachers, ministry leaders, and both male and female servants for continuance of its greatness in the world.

Chapter 2
Questions for Reflection and Discussion

1. If so, in what way do you believe that secular education institutions think that their understanding of leadership is superior to that of Christian education institutions?

2. In your own words, why should the Church be or not be considered a business?

3. What's the significance of Jesus' knowledge of the workings of business and the workplace?

4. In what way can the Gospel be equated with or described as being a "product" or not?

5. What is the relevance of the church being a worldwide enterprise?

Chapter 3
Leading as an Elder, Bishop, Shepherd, Pastor, Overseer
"The ball is in your court, if you want to lead"

Greatest Business Leadership begins with a Biblical Eldership

Tracing the history of New Testament church leadership, God initially gave the church apostles and prophets. These leaders did the foundational work after the birth of the Church (Ephesians 2:20; 4:11). As the church grew, the apostles handed the baton of leadership to elders. Elders were appointed for each church (Acts 11:23; 15:6, 23; 20:17, 28). These men were given responsibility to shepherd and oversee local churches (1 Peter 5:1-4). The New Testament reveals a pattern in which each local Church was placed under the spiritual care of a plurality of godly leaders called Elders (Strauch, 1995).

In (Acts 11:30), is realized for the first time Elders in the church. No explanation is given as to how, but they were in the early church. This is because the eldership structure of government was well known to the Hebrew Christian. Philippians 1:1 is the only passage that clearly identifies the leadership as including elders and deacons. Both elders and deacons are referred to again in (1Timothy 3). This chapter is devoted solely to the qualities and qualifications of those on the leadership team. In the New Testament, an elder, a bishop or a pastor is the same person. Titus 1:5 and 7 provide an important connection between elder and overseer. 1 Peter 5 provides the connection between elder and pastor and in verse 2, where Peter, speaking to the elders, encouraged the elders to pastor (shepherd) the flock. All three terms are grouped in (Acts 20:17) where it is recorded the apostle Paul sent for the elders of Ephesus. Upon arriving in Miletus, Paul meets these men and while speaking with them (verse 28); he refers to them as overseers and commands them to "shepherd" the congregation. These three terms are used interchangeably in the New Testament for the same individual – elder, overseer, and shepherd or "pastor." The term elder refers to the man, and overseer and shepherd refer to his function (Getz, 2003).

Functional or Dysfunctional

Elders are to be Bible men in character and knowledge. Any shortcoming of elders in Christian character and lack of knowledge of the Scriptures will have its effect on the church. "As goes the elders, so goes the church". Elders have the most solemn and serious responsibility of any group of men on earth. The awesome responsibility of the President of the United States cannot compare with the responsibility of elders. The physical, economic, and political welfare of citizens is no

comparison to the responsibility of eternity (Getz, et al., 2003).
- Elders are responsible to see that a lost world has the opportunity to hear the Gospel and the invitation of Jesus to come into the kingdom (Ephesians 3:9-11).
- Elders are charged with the responsibility of seeing that souls in the kingdom are properly fed, so that they are prepared to go to heaven (Acts 20:28; Hebrew 13:7, 17).

Another term used for elders is bishop, a term which means overseer, in Acts 20:28 it says "Take heed therefore unto yourselves, and to all the flock, over which the Holy Ghost hath made you overseers, to feed the church of God, which he hath purchased with his own blood". As overseers, the responsibility is great; they must ensure that the church is fed properly; that is, that it is taught the truth. They are to be a good example to the flock that they have the oversight of (1Peter 5:2-3). They must gladly accept their role of being entrusted with the souls of others (Hebrews 13:17). They must deal with the disorderly as well as exhort and encourage. This indeed is a great undertaking, but how honorable!

Dr. Lynn Anderson, in his book "They Smell like Sheep" (1997), discusses several views concerning leadership that represents a distorted model of leadership, that's foreign to the Bible model of a Shepherd. He shares the story of a tour guide while on one of his trips to Jerusalem, where he said, "the guide told us that he had been agitated after watching a man throwing rocks at a herd of sheep, that he jumped down off the bus, ran into the field, and accosted the man, "Do you understand what you have just done to me"? He asked. "I was spinning a charming story about the gentle ways of Shepherd's, and here you are mistreating, hazing, and assaulting these sheep! What is going on?" the man replied, "Man you've got me all wrong. I'm not a shepherd, I'm a butcher!" I thought to myself, man, what a misunderstanding there is when it comes to styles of leadership (Anderson, et al., 1997).

Faulty Models of Leadership

Dr. Anderson also talks about how several distorted leadership models find their way into modern-day churches. The first model is the Hired Hand model. However, Jesus corrects this distorted view in John chapter 10. He is only there to earn wages for that day; the hired hand has no real interest in the sheep. The next model is the Cowboy model. The difference is shepherds lead; and cowboy drives the herd, by shouting and cracking the whip. And then there is the Sheriff model. "I wear the badge and carry a gun, now move." And let's not forget the CEO/Chairman model. No real face to face contact, only memos and evaluations, nothing personal, just announce the cut-backs; and retreat to the office. Neither of these models is ideal for the church when compared to the true nature of Shepherd-Leadership modeling.

Earlier in Dr. Anderson's book he describes Biblical Shepherding as a "Relational" behavior between the Shepherd and the sheep. "Ancient, Middle-Eastern shepherds lived in the pasture with the flock and were as much a part of the land as the sheep were". Through a lifetime of shared experience, shepherds nurtured enduring trust relationships with their sheep. This relationship required availability, commitment, and trust. Since the Bible uses in (Acts 20:17-28) the terms Elders and Shepherds are interchangeable, what is to be said of the two? Dr. Anderson says that, first and foremost, "Elders are shepherds", and Shepherds are those who have flocks. Shepherds in Bible days were not day laborers who showed up for work in the morning at a stranger's pasture, put in eight hours, and then went back home; rather they lived with the sheep. In fact, through long-time and frequent touch, the shepherds smell like sheep. Elders are also mentors, persons who have walked over the trail ahead of us, a long time in the same direction. They show us how to live. And when we want to give up, they give us the courage to continue on. Elders are also equippers. They prepare Christians to do works of service. Through one-on-one time with both problems and possibilities people they guide, each may fine his or her own spiritual gift. The equippers train each member with skills needed to do his or specific ministry. As a whole, Elders are to be men of experience, character, and vision. There is a great need for elders in the church today. The fact that the church is not an ecclesial system with a human head and man-made laws does not mean there is no system or organization (Anderson, et al., 1997). Amen!

Any group of people that accomplishes anything must be organized. There must be someone to take the lead and make decisions. Therefore, these are the challenges of leading in the world's greatest business, the Church.

Chapter 3
Questions for Reflection and Discussion

1. In what way(s) is the New Testament pattern for church leadership an optional matter for the church of today?

2. Explain, in your own words, why there is a misunderstanding of the phrases Elder, Bishop, Pastor, and Shepherd, as they apply to church government today.

3. How do you interpret and apply 1Timothy 5:17, as it relates to having a full-time paid Elder who is also a preacher?

4. Dr. Anderson mentions five models of leadership: the cowboy, the hired-hand, the sheriff, the CEO-Chairman, and the Shepherd-leader; which would you apply to yourself and why?

Chapter 4
Leading as a Deacon

"If you want to lead, then drink the water first

The pattern of church leadership that the New Testament follows finds its seeds in the earliest period. In (Acts 6:1-6), we read of the frustration of some members of the early church for not having their needs attended to. Because the church had grown so large, the twelve apostles were not able to handle all the physical needs of the body and proclaim the Word too. They knew that if they neglected the ministry of the Word - the church would suffer: "It is not right for us to give up preaching the Word of God to serve tables" (v 2). They asked the congregation to choose seven men—men of good reputation and sound character—to perform this task of serving tables. Is it significant that the church only added deacons/special servants once it reached a certain size? Is it significant that the congregation took part in who should serve the tables? Is it significant that only men were chosen in Acts 6? The "Seven" were not deacons in the sense of official deacons. As realized in (Acts 8:5-37; 21:8), they were "servants" in a special work but not permanent officers in the Church (Myers, 2003).

Who will take the Job?

In Philippians 1:1, Paul addresses the saints at Philippi "together with the bishops and deacons." Thus, a twofold division of leadership is clearly seen. (1Timothy 3:1-13) addresses two categories of leaders in the church, bishops (elders) and deacons. We have already noted the connection between this text and Acts 6. Suffice it to say here that deacons were assumed to be part of the leadership of the church at Ephesus. Thus, Deacons are leaders and they are those who hold an office of service in the church that have a special responsibility to set an example for the whole church. This means if someone serves in leadership he must be willing to make the necessary commitment that leadership demands. Leaders who fail in their example have a very negative impact on the rest of the church and community (Myers, et al., 2003). Deacons are not the same as Elders. Elders are described as overseers and shepherds of the church and Deacons; the qualifications are different. In the early church certain men held this office, as in Philippians 1:1 a clear distinction was made of them and other members of the church. Deacons symbolize the heart of Christianity-Servant-hood (Matt. 20:25-28). In English, the term Deacon is translated, servant, minister, waiter or attendant. When I think of a deacon as a leader, Jesus is the first person that comes to mind. "Calling them to Himself, Jesus said to them, you know that those who are recognized as rulers of the Gentiles lord it over them; and their great men exercise authority over them. But it is not this way among you, but whosoever wishes to become great among you shall be your servant, and whosoever wishes to be first among you shall be a slave of all. For even the Son of Man did not come to be served, but to serve..." (Mark 10:42-45, NASB). Furthermore, the term deacon's literal meaning is "He who executes the commands of others." Deacons stand between elders and members. They carry out responsibilities from elders to and through members. Deacons are in rapport with elders and members. Deacons create and sustain a climate of trust between elders and members! It was the growth and development of the needs in the church that demanded these publicly recognized servants (Myers, et al., 2003). These men were given delegated authority from the bishops to do what they are qualified to do in service to the church.

- It may be overseeing the benevolent work
- Handling the finances of the church
- Heading up the visitation ministry
- Maintaining church records and the worship meeting place
- He may be the designate pulpit preacher for the church or even the evangelist

What will be their compensation?

According to 1Timothy chapter three and verse thirteen states, "For they that used the office of deacon well purchase to themselves a good degree, and great boldness in the faith which is in Christ Jesus. Aubrey Johnson, in his book "Dynamic Deacons" (2014) list five terms that identify the function of Deacons. 1) His role is being a selfless leader who serves the church, a steady leader who supports his elders, and a spiritual leader who shows Christ-likeness. 2) The requirements he must meet is to be reverent, not double-tongued, not given to much wine, not greedy for money, holding the mystery of the faith and tested. 3) His responsibility is to get clear instructions, get going – no form of procrastination, get help – not ashamed to ask and get results – the job will be done. 4) He is to have a good relationship with God, with his family, with his elders and with his peers. 5) His reward is receiving a good reputation from God. Deacon are "Trusted Lieutenants who carry out the instructions of their shepherds: servants, waiting-men, ministers" (Johnson, 2014). Therefore, when properly equipped with Deacons, some of the murmuring of the church will be stopped, most of the needs of the church can get meet, the word of the Lord will increase and the body will grow, and the Deacons will themselves grow in service, faith and assurance. Therefore, if you are serving in the capacity of deacon, recognize it an honor to be leading in the world's greatest business, the Church.

Chapter 4
Questions for Reflection and Discussion

1. In your own words, what is the significance of having Deacons?

2. In what way(s) is the Deacon to be an example to the flock?

3. Why is it important to know that a man may serve life-long as a Deacon and never become an elder?

4. Why is it important for a deacon's wife and children to be faithful?

5. What is the relationship between a deacon and his elders?

Chapter 5
Leading as a Preacher/ Evangelist
"If you want to lead then learn to serve"

These things speak.....Titus 2:15

Now, what about the Preacher? Let's talk about him! The picture of Preachers in the New Testament is a Leader. Does this reject the concept of Elders leading the local church? Certainly not! They are Shepherds, overseers, and Bishops, which gives them the right to decision-making in the local body, the church (Acts 20:28; 1 Peter 5:1-5). Does it promote the Preacher as the "Pastor" of the church? No! For this isn't what the New Testament teaches and isn't what we should do. Preachers should be the kind of servant leaders who exalt Christ and promote the growth of the church by taking a leadership role as God's servant.

We are at a section in this book where we want to discuss the Preacher/Evangelist's role as a leader. Ironically, there is research that suggests that in growing churches, stress was placed on the leadership ability and work of the Preacher. It ranked as third in importance in growing churches behind preaching and evangelism. While in declining churches the leadership of the preacher ranked as seventh place in importance (Malphurs, 2004). In our discussion let's say that: Evangelists were included with the apostles, prophets, pastors, and teachers (Ephesians 4:11). Apostles and prophets had to do with temporary, miraculous work that Christ gifted men to do. But evangelist, pastors, and teachers were all men whom Christ gifted in non-miraculous ways and that their work is one which continues as long as this world continues. The effects of the work of the apostles and prophets won't stop either. Instead of the preacher/evangelist and pastors being pictured in some hierarchal position, the Holy Spirit led Paul to picture them both functioning as partners working to fulfill a single mission for those who are in the body of Christians. As the Body we must work together to equip the saints, to work in ministry, so the body of Christ may be matured.

…..And by What Authority?

Paul wrote to Timothy and Titus, preachers who were not apostles or elders but were an Evangelist, serving as preachers where there were elders in the church. In Timothy's case, there had been elders in Ephesus for a long time. Paul wrote to instruct Timothy to remain in Ephesus and charge some "to teach no other doctrine" (1Timothy 1:3). He told him what kind of man to look for in appointing additional men as Shepherds and Servants in the congregation. Paul warned the leadership of apostasy in the church by those who would bind things which God had not bound and told him to instruct the brethren in these things. He told him to live what he preached. He told him not to take into the number who were not "truly widows." If they had a family, they should take care of them. He told him to honor elders who led well, "especially those who labor in word and teaching." This, of course, had reference to paying one who was preaching and teaching as an Elder (1Timothy 5:1-19). He was told not to accept accusations against an Elder except before two or three witnesses. Do all things without prejudice and don't lay hand suddenly on any man. This seems to do with appointing men as elders. The fact it was written to Timothy indicates he has some charge concerning church matters.

In reference to what Paul said to Titus, who was to "Set in order the thing which were lacking and appoint elders in every city". It is important to understand that men are not qualified because they are appointed, but appointed because they are qualified. We also note that the inspired admonition was that elders were to be appointed in every city, bolstered by Paul's making it clear that this was an apostolic command. The phrases every church, every city, makes it abundantly evident that elders are to preside in every congregation of the Lord's church. The Preacher was to teach sound doctrine, which was to tell people of all ages how to live and get involved with the work of the church. In Paul's letter to Titus, it addresses three particular topics: church organization, holy living, and discipline (Titus 1-3). In my opinion, one the most profound and challenging set of standards for the preacher-evangelist is found in (1Timothy 4:12-16).

¹²" Let no man look down upon thy youth; but be thou an ensample to them that believe, in word, in manner of life, in love, in faith, in purity. ¹³ Till I come, give heed to reading, to exhortation, to teaching. ¹⁴ Neglect not the gift that is in thee, which was given thee by prophecy, with the laying on of the hands of the presbytery. ¹⁵ Be diligent in these things; give thyself wholly to them; that thy progress may be manifest unto all. ¹⁶ Take heed to thyself, and to thy teaching. Continue in these things; for in doing this thou shalt save both thyself and them that hear thee" (ASV).

Certainly, as today's workforce climate calls for moral living among leaders of all disciplines, these instructions have to be among the highest standards of any. Therefore, modeling a New Testament pattern as preachers and evangelists is no small task. While Paul's letters to Timothy and Titus do not teach that the preachers were the chief leaders in the churches where they work, they certainly teach that they were leaders and powerful ones at that.

Why continue to Preach? Romans 10:14

In response, I believe it has to do with Christian Vocation and Self-Leadership, and living what I truly believed in. The idea of Christian vocation reminds me of the many years of being bi-vocational, a term used in association with being in both Ministry and pursing a secular career. Unfortunately, in today's career-obsessed world, many people associate vocation with the career. If someone was to ask you what is your vocation, you would respond by telling them what you did for a living; in other words, your profession. However, this is not the accurate use of the word. According to Greek lexicons, the term "vocation" is from the Latin word "vocare" which literally means "to call" and "kaleo" from the Greek, means "to call or to summon." The idea of calling caused me to ponder what this calling is. My conclusion is that one's vocation/calling is to be of a divine origin, what one has a passion for doing whether compensated or not. On the other hand, a career is what you do to make a living. The concept of Christian vocation/calling has been my greatest inner challenge. It has caused me at times to choose between having a career to make some "real" money, or solely develop myself to the highest caliber in order to serve in ministry. Even though, I possess the skills to be economically successful and serve in the ministry as well, I believe that this is where self- leadership plays a major role in directing my ambitions and causing me to trust God to promote me economically.

Furthermore, Christian vocation/calling has influenced my decision to aspire to be a great leader and a teacher of leadership. Self-leadership has challenged me to question at least two things about myself. (1) Whether my heart for God is increasing and deepening? (2) Is my pace for ministry sustainable? I wonder at times of how that an increased heart and a deepening love is properly determined in light of the scriptures. My sustainability concern is a bit different in that I am challenged to settle for a pace that is compatible with those who follow my lead, which at times appears to be counterproductive personally. It seems at times that I am not on track to get where I believe God wants me to be in the world's greatest business, the Church. Fortunately, I have to this point in life, stayed the course. Therefore, being a preacher-evangelist in the world's greatest business, the Church is no small thing. It's both challenging and rewarding, it's an honor!

Chapter 5
Questions for Reflection and Discussion

1. What is your view as to how a person is called to become a Preacher or an Evangelist?

2. How do you reconcile the majority of churches that refers to their Preacher as the "Pastor" of their church, when it seems to differ from the New Testament pattern?

3. In what way(s) has church members become confused with the hiring a man as an Evangelist, that never travels anywhere preaching the Gospel?

4. In your opinion, is it appropriate for the local preacher to also become one the bishops/elders of the congregation?

5. What are the qualifications to become a Preacher?

Chapter 6
Teacher as a Leader
"If you want to lead, you must like to read"

Go ye therefore, and teach…(Matthew 28:19)
In the world, there are many types of teachers. There are teachers in public schools at every level, from childhood through college age. For every job, there are teachers who can teach others to perform that special task or service. But when we speak of teachers in this context, we are not talking about teachers in the world system of education. We are speaking of teachers God sets in the Church and of the teaching task of believers. The church is fundamentally a teaching-learning organization. Its future depends on the effectiveness of its leaders and members as they function as both teacher and learners (Bredfelt, 2006). If the process of teaching is lost, the church will have paid a steep price for its material successes (Colossians 1:28-29); because by nature, the church is a teaching–learning organization. Teachers have great influence and can bring about great change.

"And God hath set some in the church,
first apostles, secondarily prophets,
thirdly teachers" (I Corinthians 12:28).

The word "teach" means to instruct, show,

demonstrate, inform, impart knowledge, train and guide the studies of another. A "teacher" is one who teaches. "Teaching" is the act of instructing and training others. Teaching and preaching by true believers are the methods God has chosen to reach the nations with the Gospel. The idea of a leader being responsible for developing a learning organization brings to mind the admonition of which the Apostle Paul gave to the Evangelists Timothy and Titus (2Timothy 2:2; Titus 1:5). To Timothy, he said, "Teach the things that you have learned from me unto faithful men, who will, in turn, teach the same thing to other men". This directive calls for a place and time to be executed. The learning opportunities that were set in place by a teacher/leader will in time perpetuate knowledge and progress. To Titus, he said, set things in order, things that are lacking, and ordain elders in every city. These elders were to become the teachers and decision makers of the church (1 Timothy 5:17-19). In essence, leaders of any organization must be informed leaders if they would lead effectively. In today's terms, whether it is in churches or corporations or organizations; whenever there are ongoing teaching and learning, this is a learning centre. As it was with Titus and Timothy, leaders of today must extend or duplicate their abilities to multiple levels by teaching others what they have learned through experience and through academics. They should be motivated by the changing trends and fads in the market-place (Marquardt, 2011). At the most basic core of biblical leadership is one indispensable, unchanging function of the Christian leader---the task of teaching God's Word with clarity, in its original context, and in a way that is relevant to those whose hearts are open to hearing. The Biblical leader is first and foremost a Bible teacher, and the people of God are a distinctive teaching-learning community where the principles of business leadership may not always apply (Bredfelt, et al., 2006).

Power equals Influence!

Teachers have enormous influence, long after they depart from the earth, their words and ideas continue on and to have a life-changing impact. Teaching is an enormous responsibility because it is an extremely powerful method of leadership. In fact, when it comes to leading the people of God, it is the most powerful means of bringing genuine and lasting change (Bredfelt, et al., 2006). In the case of the Ethiopian eunuch a [leader] in (Acts 8:26-40). This man was at the right spiritual place. He was in Jerusalem where the great temple of worship was located (Acts 8:27). He was there for the right purpose. He had come to worship (Acts 8:27). He was reading the right book. He was reading a portion of God's Word in (Isaiah 53:7; Acts 8:30). But he still needed someone to help Him understand. He needed a teacher. God sent Philip to instruct him. The eunuch accepted the Gospel and was baptized in water. Without teachers, unsaved people are like sheep without a shepherd. They do not understand which way to go (Mark 6:34). Even believers have problems and without proper teaching, God said...MY PEOPLE are destroyed for lack of knowledge (Hosea 4:6).

Understanding the Times

As we speak about leading in the greatest business in the world, we must also consider the future of the churches of Christ, the greatest business in the world, as we know it. Twenty to thirty years from now, what will the church look like? Considering the changing of worldview about things, how will this affect the church? Phil. 2:15...says that we should "shine as lights in the world". Will we have the faith and strength to withstand the war that is being waged against the faith? The Bible teaches that the church is to educate the world about God (Eph. 3:11). Will the church stay the course? Or will it be absorbed in the culture shift? What will it take to sustain ourselves? I believe that if one knows what's going on, they will know what to do. The text of (1 Chronicles 12:32) tells us that those men of God were very informed men, who knew what was best for their people. They were perhaps weather-wise, a breasted of the public affairs; they had a hand on the pulse of the nation and the tendencies of the present events of those days, (Luke 1:3; 2:27). It will take men and women of the Lord's church to understand the times, in order to sustain ourselves in our present world situation. There are three things that sustain a society,cultures, and nations; a language, the way it communicates; reasoning, the way it thinks and a behavior, the way it acts (Gen 11:1-12).

Change is Upon Us

The language of today is changing (Neh. 13:23). We once had a clear meaning of what things meant. It is believed that our young people will be more affected by these changes in language because of their constant exposure to the internet and social media, technology and less Bible and spiritual information (Eph. 6:4; Titus 2:3-4; Eph. 5:1-7). The way people reason today has changed and is yet changing – (Proverbs 14:12; 16:25). Our world's behavior of today is changing – (Judges 17:6). Unless we realize that righteousness exalts a nation, we will constantly change our language, our reasoning and our behaviors. Leaders of the church must stay an abreast of the shifting cultures, the hidden languages of change, that wars against the faith. Thus, leaders in this great business of saving souls must understand the times. It is very comforting to know that the greatest of leaders among us are not powerful senior executives, commanding military strategists, celebrated athletics coaches, or respected political figures. No the greatest leaders among us are the great teachers among us. In many ways, and in different areas, great teachers, influence through their passion, their character, and their words. Teachers shape, challenge and change people and in doing so, they lead (Bredfelt, et al., 2006). Great teachers are leaders, and conversely, great leader must be teachers.

Every believer is to teach (Deuteronomy 6:6-7; Matthew 28:19-20; 2 Timothy 2:2-4; Hebrews 5:12). We teach two main groups of people: ALL NATIONS and FAITHFUL MEN. Each person taught is to teach others who are also able to teach. This is the pattern of continuous teaching that rapidly multiplies to spread the Gospel throughout the w o r l d . Greatest business teachers must stay a breasted of the times. Therefore, if you serve in the capacity of a teacher, consider it an honor to lead in the world's greatest business, the Church.

Chapter 6
Questions for Reflection and Discussion

1. In your own words, explain how being a teacher in the church is considered as Leadership.

2. The author mentioned that a teacher has enormous influence; how can you apply this fact to your own leadership ability and context?

3. Why is it important to have an understanding of the times, in order to be an effective teacher?

4. Based on your observation or experience, do you think that teachers in their work as teachers, in relationship to the work of preaching is inferior? If so, or not so, then why?

Chapter 7
As a Ministry Leader
"If you want to lead, then give the people directions to follow"

A Theology of Ministry

First and foremost, when we speak of Ministry, what do we mean? Do we mean something that man decides to do or do we mean something that God decides to do through man? Is this all about me or is this all about God? If it is about God, then the foundation and motivation must begin with God. The Apostle Paul instructs Timothy in (2 Timothy 3:16-17), "All scripture is given by inspiration of God, and is profitable for doctrine, for reproof, for correction, for instruction in righteousness: that the man of God may be perfect, thoroughly furnished unto all good works". This is to say that the man of God's work will be founded upon the scriptures, and its guidelines are from scripture, in others words; his ministry is to be based on the Bible. Also in (2Timothy 4:4), he is told to "make full proof of thy ministry." Note: this ministry does belong to Timothy, but he works for God. Also notice that ministry is designed to save both the minister and those who hear him, (1 Timothy 4:16). Therefore, everything that this ministry consists of must include biblical principles, guidelines, and moralities. By doing this your ministry becomes authoritative, because it's from God.

Serious questions need to be asked before one pursues ministry. Why are we here? What is to be done? How is it to be done? And how important is it to us? I believe that these four questions should be the framework to all ministries. These four questions can be presented as Purpose, Mission, Vision and Value statements. They provide a track to run on and allow endless possibilities. If it is our ultimate goal to go to heaven and be with God and others, then we must utilize the source and resources that will enable us to get there. The Apostle Peter states, that God "according to his divine power hath given unto us all things that pertain to life and godliness," (2Peter 1:3a). If we are truly people of the book, people of the Bible, then why not use the book, the Bible as our primary guide and source? We can't do biblical things from outside of the Bible, and expect biblical outcomes. Therefore ministry must be biblical.

Your Theology Matters

Whatever you believe about ministry will dictate your actions. Therefore, one's philosophy is the key factor in determining the makeup and outcome of their ministry. If my philosophy is flawed and/or un-biblical; I am certain to miss the mark and the expectations of God. With that in mind, Ministry Leadership resides in the person more than the process. This principle is found throughout Scripture. Leaders in the Bible led because of their relationship with God, not because they were expert managers. Ministry leadership is thus a matter of personal spiritual maturity and growth (2Peter 3:18). Christians are attracted to spiritually mature people and responsive to their influence. Those whom God calls to Ministry Leadership, first is called to spiritual maturity.

Ministry Leaders work more through influence (role-modeling) than power (formal authority). People follow them because they want to, not because they have to. Therefore, Ministry Leadership is not tied only to positions of formal authority—it is not job specific. Since Christ's model of leadership is based on sacrificial service to others, Christian leaders expect to serve rather than to be served. This requires that we subordinate our own needs and attend to the needs of others. Ministry leaders are able to build themselves into others because of the overflow of their spiritual blessings. Those who have the most, serve the most (Luke 12:48).

Taking Your Place in Ministry

So often when the church makes strong efforts to involve the flock in church work, many members are known to say; "If I had a talent or a gift I would gladly get involved." What many fail to realize is that they already have the talent or gift needed to get involved. Consider what you do to make a living and bear in mind, God will not ask you if he did not think you could do it (Romans 12:5-8). For example, if you are a Salesperson, then you are a talker and persuader, thus you will be a good fit for the greeting, inviting, and teaching and evangelism ministries. If you are a Counselor, you are a good listener and advisor, you will be good at comforting and crisis intervention and grief work. If you are a Teacher, you are an instructor and motivator; you will be good in educating, mentoring and lesson plan development. If in Customer service, you are a people person, you would do well as a greeter. Medical Professional, you are caring and sacrificial, you will work well in nursing home visits and providing wellness information. In Food-service, you like to serve people; you will do well with fellowship meals and in-home get together. In Administration, you like organization and communication; you will do well in clerical, and ministry coordination. Management, Banking and Finance, all of these prepare you to assist the leadership in church management. Landscaping and Housekeeping go hand in hand with building and grounds upkeep.

    Look, God knows your place in the kingdom; he is preparing you while you earn a living. To better make my point, let's take a look at the Evangelism Ministry Leader and his leadership. The work of the church has often been described as threefold: Edification – equipping the saints for ministry, Benevolence – meeting the needs of destitute brethren and Evangelism – spreading the good news of Jesus Christ to the lost. The organization and worship of the local church naturally focus attention on Edification – the office of elders (pastors) speaks to the work of building up the saints, Benevolence – the office of deacons along with weekly contribution speak to supplying the needs of the saints. Unless frequent attention is given to Evangelism, it can become easy for churches to focus solely on edification and benevolence and neglect evangelistic efforts both as a congregation and as individuals. Tragically, to neglect evangelism is harmful to the spiritual life of the church. Let's ask God to forgive us if we have been neglecting this important duty. Note this, "without effective leadership there will be no need for evangelism, and without evangelism there will be no need for leadership"

Ministry leaders must have a "big picture" perceptive of the church in order to be an effect ministry leader. Neither a church, nor any organization can ever be larger or greater than its leadership; in fact, a church's success is determined by the effectiveness of its leadership. Each ministry of the church must have strong leadership. Therefore, if you serve in the church in any capacity consider it an honor to lead in the world's greatest business, the Church.

Chapter 7
Questions for Reflection and Discussion

1. In what way do you find it difficult to pursue a leadership role in the church when you are not recognized as an elder, deacon, or a preacher?

2. How are you affected by having to make more than normal sacrifices once you become a ministry leader?

3. Explain how being a ministry leader is as important as being an official leader of the church such as a deacon or a preacher?

4. How can you best develop yourself to become an effective leader of a ministry?

Chapter 8
Women Role in Church Leadership

"If you want to lead, then first enlighten them"

Diamonds in the Rough

Women were prominent in many activities in the early church and during the Old Testament era. These activities included prophesying (Acts 2:17-18), claiming the fulfillment of (Joel 2: 28-29); teaching (Titus 2:3-5; Acts 18:26) and working in the advancing of the Gospel; however, the details are unspecified (Philippians 4:3; Rom. 16:1-2, 6-7, 12). During Jesus' public ministry women provided financial support for him and the disciples (Luke 8:1-3). After the church began we can notice that Sister Dorcas was devoted to good works and acts of charity (Acts 9:36). And without any doubt, Phoebe had apostolic endorsement of her ministry, whatever it may have been (Romans 16:1, 2).

"We must confess that churches have not always utilized women as fully as the scriptures indicated they were involved in apostolic days. In reflecting cultural norms of the past, the church through history has sometimes not only failed to put women to work fully but has even allowed their repression. The cultural setting will certainly influence the extent to which women are involved, but cultural practice and societal preference should not lead the church into either error, either placing undue restrictions on women's work or not respecting Biblical limitations" (Ferguson, 2001).

Women held a leading place in the Christian society, particularly the women in the region of Macedonia. In Macedonia: they were the first to be preached to (Acts 16:11-14) and the first to show hospitality to Preachers (Acts 16:15). In Philippi: women of Business (Acts 16:14). In Thessalonica: women in Chief roles in government (Acts 17:34); In Athens: first in conversion and in Berea: women of honor (Acts 17:10-12). It is my understanding of the scriptures and my deepest conviction, that the only limitation of women in the church assembly, is to have teaching and leading authority over the males in the public assembly meetings (1Timothy 2:10-15).

Shining as Lights in the World

It is evident that the Apostle Paul had a good working relationship with women and probably because of it, the women in the church at Philippi may have influenced the church there to financially support him when no other church would (Philippians 4:15).The two women: Euodias and Syntyche were evidently influential members of the church; they were "Ladies of Rank" who displayed an active zeal for the cause of Christ. They were deserving women, they labored in the Gospel with Paul and he remembered their good deeds (Ferguson, et al., 2001). Women did much for Christ in the Philippians church and women can do much in the church of today. Their ability to lead is unquestionable and they should lead other women in becoming good teachers of ladies classes, especially the older teaching the younger (Titus 2:3-4). Women have immense influence as an instructor of children. They can do one-on-one studies pointed toward converting especially women who are not Christians; to include males (Acts 18:26). They can lead as supervisor of children classes more effectively than the male because of her natural gift in raising children (1 Timothy 2:15). They may lead in organizing fellowship activities and in a hundred other things and therefore, render great service as a part of the local congregation.

Is it cultural?

Unfortunately, there is still that question of whether women can or should be "Pastors or Preachers" and if not then why not? Women are of equal importance as the man, for God values people for their service not their authority. In particular, the women's role as a homemaker is of great value. Women have a definite responsibility in teaching (Titus 2:2-3). However, the Bible draws a connection between the home and the church. Just as there is a role distinction at home—where the husband is called to lead the family—there is also one at church, the assembly. At home, men are proving their fitness to be elders (pastors), and at church, they are the ones who are given that role (1Timothy 3:4-5). It's not a problem for a woman to minister in hundreds of ways in the church, but the office of leadership and teaching of men is preserved for spiritual and godly men (Strauch, 1995).

Another question along this line is why didn't Jesus choose women as some of his apostles? The Twelve are all men. That was intentional, because they are all given incredible authority to found the Church. They are like pastors, only they have more authority than pastors. But Jesus did call women, and he called them into significant ministry. It was counter-cultural to have Mary sitting at his feet learning like a rabbinic student at the feet of his teacher. But he did not choose women to be apostles (Myers, 2003). That wasn't because he was enslaved to his times/culture. It was because, in coherence with the rest of the Bible (Genesis 1-2, Ephesians 5, 1 Corinthians 11, and 1 Timothy 2), he believed that it would be healthy for the church and the family if men assumed the role of Christ-like, humble, caring, servant-leaders, and if the women came in alongside with their respective gifts to help carry his leadership through according to those gifts. It is not about abilities, but rather it is about roles (Galatians 3:28). God has ordained that in the home and in the church, for males to assume a special role of responsible leadership and teaching (Strauch, et al., 1995). Women, you are not handcuffed, so therefore lead! And, if you serve in the church in any capacity consider it an honor to lead in the world's greatest business, the church.

Chapter 8
Questions for Reflection and Discussion

1. In your own words, how can the church more efficiently use women in the leadership functions of the church?

2. To what degree has the role of the older women been diminished in the church and why?

3. How creative can a church become when a woman has the gift of speaking and teaching that's far superior to any male in the church?

4. Explain whether the supposing suppression of women's role in the church today is a cultural issue or a theological one?

Chapter 9
Modeling Leadership (Acquiring)

"You can push from behind, but not lead from behind"

As earlier stated Leadership is an inevitable calling and can be acquired through many avenues. You may already be in leadership and do a good job of leading, but good leaders are always striving to become even better ones. Leadership appears to be glamorous but is more often lonely and thankless. After spending nearly ten years in the Army, I acquired (military leadership), employed in insurance sells, marketing and management (corporate leadership), being active in church work for over thirty-six years (spiritual-church leadership) and (educational leadership), and as a husband and father of five children and six grand children (domestic leadership). It is noteworthy that an interest in the philosophy of leadership increased during the early part of the twentieth century. Early leadership theories focused on what qualities distinguished between leaders and followers, while subsequent theories looked at other variables such as situational factors and skill levels (Northouse, 2013).

Just exactly who are you?

While many different leadership theories have emerged, most can be classified as of one of eight major types: Great Man Theories: Great man theories assume that the capacity of leadership is inherent – that great leaders are born not made. These men by nature are destined to rise to leadership. Trait Theories: Similar in some ways to "Great Man" theories, trait theories assume that people inherit certain qualities and traits that make them better suited to leadership. Trait theories often identify a particular personality or behavioral characteristics shared by leaders. Contingency Theories: Contingency theories of leadership focus on particular variables related to the environment that might determine which particular style of leadership is best suited for the situation. According to this theory, no leadership style is best in all situations. Situational Theories: This theory proposes that leaders choose the best course of action based on situational variables. Different styles of leadership may be more appropriate for certain types of decision-making. Behavioral Theories: Behavioral theories are based on the belief that great leaders are made, and not born. Rooted in behaviorism, this leadership theory focuses on the actions of leaders, not on mental qualities or internal states. According to this theory, people can learn to become great leaders. Participative Theories: Participative leadership theories suggest that the ideal leadership style is one that takes the input of others into account.

These leaders encourage participation and contribution from group members and help group members feel more relevant and committed to the decision-making process. In this, the leader retains the right to allow the input of others. Management Theories: Management theories, also known as transitional theories, focus on the role of supervision, organization and group performance. Managerial theories are often used in business; when employees are successful, they are rewarded; when they fail, they are punished or reprimanded. Relationship Theories: Relationship theories, also known as transformational theories, focus upon the connections formed between leaders and followers. Transformational leaders motivate and inspire people by helping group members see the importance and higher good of the task. Leaders with this style often have high ethical and moral standard (Northouse, et al., 2013). Question! Are you more confused now than before? Just what kind of leader are you or did you think you were or would like to become?

The Man, the Mission?

According to the (Great Man) theory, a man is born with these qualities and according to (Behavioral), he must learn these qualities or he can be taught them. In contrast to Great man and Behavioral theories as to men becoming leaders, is that leaders in the world's greatest business, the Church, are made by the Holy Spirit. Yes, the Holy

Spirit makes men overseers (Acts 20:28). The way that the Holy Spirit makes elders is by the Bible which is the sword of the Spirit (Ephesians 6:17). The Holy Spirit inspired the Scriptures which provide the teaching that makes men elders in the church. Christianity is a taught religion (John 6:45). Believers are taught before baptism and taught after baptism (Matthew 28:19, 20). The qualifying and selecting of elders require much long and careful teaching. As a man learns the characteristics of a mature Christian he strives to attain them. He develops a strong desire to be a strong Christian, able to help others to follow Christ. In this way, the Holy Spirit is bringing forth fruits of Christian character (Galatians 5:22, 23). Qualified men must be chosen out of the congregation so as to be considered in view of possible selection. Notice that this step is for the congregation to take. The whole church, after proper teaching, is to search out from its own members those mature men who meet the requirements to be officers (1Timothy 3:1-5). The Bible says that elders are to be ordained or appointed (Titus 1:5, Acts 14:23). After elders have been considered, approved, and appointed by the congregation, there remains only the recognizing of the new officers by the church.

Theoretically Speaking!

As afore-mentioned, there have been thousands of books and articles written; workshop, seminars, and retreats conducted to gain a better understanding of this all-encompassing subject, leadership. Many theories have come and gone, and are coming around again, but in different forms. Men are reluctant to accept both brief and lengthy definitions and descriptions given concerning leadership because of their own ideas. As a result, there is a need for theories to be developed that help increases their understanding of the broader and often subtle contexts in which effective leadership takes place. From this realization has emerged a demand for more holistic leadership theories and practice that integrates the body (physical), mind (logical/rational thought), heart (emotions, feelings), and spirit (Moxley, 2000). In recent years, an immense focus has been given to the emergence of a spiritual leadership theory. According to Fry (2003), an organization can no longer rely solely upon previous leadership theories in order to transform learning opportunities; whereof "Spiritual leadership taps into the fundamental needs of both leader and follower for spiritual survival so they become more organizationally committed and productive" (p.694). Furthermore, spiritual leadership which compromises of values, attitudes, and behaviors, in comparison to focusing on the physical, mental, or emotional elements of humans, produce a more holistic result (Fry, et al., 2003).

Spiritually Speaking!

Chen and Yang (2012) define spiritual leadership theory as a combination of the motivation-based perspectives from previous leadership theories, transformational and charismatic leaders with the religious-based perspective. Accordingly, this theory of leadership entails: creating a vision, producing a sense of membership and feeling of being understood and appreciated and helping members develop a sense of being understood and appreciated through interrelationship (Kaya, 2015). This sounds like church-life-leadership to me! Furthermore, Spiritual leadership emerges from the interactions of altruistic love, vision, and hope/faith of organizational members. Therefore, in the theory of spiritual leadership, vision, altruistic love, and hope/faith are core to the understanding of spiritual leadership (Fry, et al., 2003). Spiritual Leadership, as literature so indicates, is founded upon godly character and values. Once spiritual leaders understand God's will, they make every effort to move their followers from following their own agendas to pursuing God's purposes (Blackaby & Blackably, 2012). People who fail to move people to God's agenda have not led. Spiritual leaders depend on the Holy Spirit. Spiritual leaders work with a paradox, for God calls them to do something that, in fact; only God can do (Sanders, 2007). Spiritual leaders are accountable to God. Spiritual leaders necessitate an acute sense of accountability. Just as a teacher has not taught until students have learned, leaders don't blame their followers when they don't do what they should do. Spiritual leaders can influence all people, not just God's people. In others words, God's agenda applies to the marketplace as well as the meeting place (church house). God can use them to exert significant godly influence upon unbelievers (Sanders, et al., 2007). When most people think of leadership, they picture a military officer giving out orders or an employer closely supervising his employees, making sure all the work gets done. These aspects can be a part of leadership, but they are not the essence of spiritual leadership. Spiritual leadership is the opposite of what most people think. Spiritual leadership is servant leadership, it involves humbling yourself and doing the tasks that no one else wants to do, its leadership with a spirit of humility and service and that causes people to follow you because they want to, not because they have to (John 10:1-13; 13:1-16).

Comparatively and practically speaking!

Spiritual leadership has commonalities with supportive, transformational, servant, and charismatic leadership theories. Supportive leadership is a kind of leadership, where you listen to your subordinates and help them out when they need help. Supportive leadership helps to build and maintain effective interpersonal relationships. If you practice supportive leadership, your people will likely be more satisfied with you and with their jobs (Yuki, 2010). Transformational leadership implies that followers respect, admire, and trust the leader and emulate his or her behavior, assume their values, and are committed to achieving their vision and making sacrifices in this regard (Northouse, 2013). Charismatic leadership refers to the leader(s) enthusiasm and optimism in creating a vision of the future, in most cases the immediate future, thus stimulating similar feelings with followers (House, 2010 & Bass, 2010). Servant leadership as described and popularized by Greenleaf (2002) consist of two roles converged into one. That is, a person is first a servant who aspires to become a leader or a leader that develops into a servant. Furthermore, the theory suggests that the leader's humility and teamwork spirit induces the follower to commit to the leader and his cause (Northouse, et al., 2013). All sounds like church-life-leadership to me! Spiritual leadership, however, supports and manifests the attributes of all four theories, which is unbelievable but also is undeniable. Too often, leadership is founded upon skill. Those with great vision, planning, organizational and communication skills are most often given leadership. Though these are critical to effective leadership, but without godly character and values, they will not produce enduring results. While spiritual leadership involves many of the same principles as general leadership, spiritual leadership has certain distinctive qualities that must be understood and practice if leaders are to be successful. God raises people up to leadership, first on the basis of character, then on the basis of skill (1Timothy 3:1-9). The spiritual leader's task is to move people from where they are to where God wants them to be. Therefore, if you serve in the church in any capacity consider it an honor to lead in the world's greatest business, the Church.

Chapter 9
Questions for Reflection and Discussion

1. Explain how Servant leadership applies to you in your context

2. Explain how Transformational leadership applies to you in your context

3. Explain how Spiritual leadership applies to you in your context

4. Explain how Charismatic leadership applies to you in your context

5. Explain how Supportive leadership applies to you in your context

Chapter 10
Modeling Leadership (The Practice)

"If you will lead, then not just manage but do something"

Is it all about Character?

According to (1Timothy 3:1-7), leadership is described as he who would become an elder, must be blameless, the husband of one wife, having faithful children not accused of riot or unruly. The idea of being blameless does not mean perfect or sinless, but refers to being without accusation, irreproachable. But it does address the need that the man who would aspire to be an elder not have uncorrected wrongs which can be leveled against him. He is to be faithful to his wife. He must have influence, control and the respect of his family. And his family must be faithful to God. It is reasonable to say that his character should be good both within the church and the local community.

In light of (1Tim.3:5-7), he must also have control over his own behavior, his attitude and his motives. He must also manage his affairs and the affairs of God's church as a good steward of someone else's things, (Acts 20: 28). He must be trusted and he cannot be self-willed. This person must love people, and be willing to help them whenever he can. He is to be a lover of good things, stable in his thinking, a just and holy man, and one that knows and love the word of God. He must have self-disciplined and able to persuade others to do the right thing for God and his fellow man (Titus 1:6, 7). Furthermore, he must be able to teach and not be a novice in the Lord (1Tim. 3:1-7).

Is it all about Skills?

According to Winkler (2003), those who study church leadership are aware of key points or factors to generally consist of nine skills. Personal (spiritual) skills: first and foremost they must know their Bibles and are able to teach the Bible. They are to have a fervent prayer life, lead a meaningful devotional life, truly know and love God, are constantly growing in their spiritual life and having lost their affection and attachment from the world. People skills: successful leaders possess, and constantly develop and improve their people skills. They are genuinely "people-persons." They are out among the sheep (John 10:4; Acts 20:18-20). They are approachable, good listeners, kind-hearted, respectful of others, have a sense of humor, have faith in people, are observant, have a concept of church life, and live a transparent life. Relational skills: they realize that no one segment of church work is exclusively subject to one leader's control. They realize that they must keep open lines of communication with other elders, deacons, preachers and ministry leaders. They realized that they must share equal burdens, duties, and responsibilities, even when they are unpleasant.

Decision making skills: indecision is a death blow to any organization, even the greatest one in the world. Elders, preacher, and deacons alike are non-function or dysfunctional if they are not able to make decisions; preferably sound ones. When making up one's mind to end a controversy, resolving a matter, determining a course of action, making a choice or rendering a verdict; leader must understand what it means and how to best carry it out. First, it should be done pray-fully, having considered others and having received biblical and sound advice. Communication skills: in great churches, there is an undisturbed flow of communications. Its leaders consistently communicate with its members and since leaders are to be approachable and available, the membership should feel free to communicate with the leaders. Problem-solving skills: in order to sustain an organization to include Christian ones; its leadership must have a proven method of problem-solving. There will be problems! Moses had many of them (Exodus 18:16). Paul and the others apostles implemented several problem-solving tragedies, and churchmen of today should model them. Time management skills: time management save lives, souls and can make or lose money. It's just great for business. Great elders make time for his family, church members, study, meetings and other important events in their life.

This skill set is a must if the church or any business would be a great one. Organizational skills: organization is a Bible principle, (Acts 6:1-7; 1 Corinthians 12:12-31). They are inherent of the appellatives applied to elders; that is, seeing that things to be done by others the righty.

A Hopeful Balance

Those who study leadership agree upon key points or factors that seem to qualify leaders as being balanced as far as character and competency are considered. However, in the world's greatest business, the Church, these same factors are common and are expected among its leaders as well. Corporate America and other disciplines alike embrace these skill sets as their benchmarks in reference to leadership performance measures (Winkler, et al., 2003). Therefore, if you serve in the church in any capacity consider it an honor to lead in the world's greatest business, the Church.

Chapter 10
Questions for Reflection and Discussion

1. Explain how time-management is having an effect on your leadership.

2. In what way(s) do you find it difficult to make tough decisions?

3. Explain how you process or develop team-building when it seems like others are disconnected from the mission.

4. Explain how you are able to stay organized in a seemingly dysfunctional environment.

Chapter 11
Modeling Leadership (Self Leadership)
"Lead the charge, but lead yourself first"

The Man - Before Leadership

Now, let's discuss the subject of Self-Leadership and its role in effective church leadership. Self-Leadership can be described as "the process of influencing oneself". It's leadership that we exercise over ourselves. If we ever hope to be effective leaders of others, we need to be able to lead ourselves effectively (Manz & Neck, 2013). The Apostle Paul states "let this mind be in you"… (Philippians 2:3-5). Thus, effective self-leadership practices are determined mostly by how we recognize the importance of what we are and how we thinks about things. In other words, we become what we tolerate. In his book "Point Man" (2003), Steve Farrar presents four interesting points regarding manhood development. He presents the man as the "point man" and designates the man as the one who "saves the boys". Farrar describes the man as "a one women kind of man" and he shows what "real men don't do". He tells us that "Satan has declared war on the family, and the way he is to defeat the family is to neutralize the man." It is therefore up to the man to combat Satan to guard the family. Poor Adam! Thus, the Lord teaches us in the gospel of Matthew that the strong man must first be bonded before one can take his goods. Furthermore, Farrar says that "a boy is the only thing that God can use to make a man." Therefore, the man is to direct the boys to God by their lives. Farrar also relates a story of burning bridges and burning ships, as the means to eliminating all options to retreat on a commitment. He says in essence, regardless of past relationships with women, you must eliminate all options of leaving your wife for other women, thus saving the boys and being a one women kind of man. Real men don't abandon their family; because his children recognize him as the Shepherd of the family.

Edwin Louis Cole in his book "Maximized Manhood" (1982) poses the question, "is there a priest in the house?" Implying that the man is to be the spiritual leader, the one who is first among others, connected with God. So then, before a man becomes a leader in the church, he must first be the leader of the home (1Timothy 3:4-5). In Acts 6:1-7, these men were proven before the church used them in church work. Fathers give the first impression of manhood. The right kind of father must first be the right kind of man. He is to take interest in his home and children by spending time with them: training, loving, disciplining, and teaching them (Ephesians 6:4; Hebrews 12:6-11). A leader's family is his laboratory for leadership, so we must serve them well and serve them often.

If done well, then we can look behind and ask, "Who's following me now?"

"Private leadership must precede Public leadership"

The great controversy of today is whether a leader's personal life and private behavior in any way germane to his public leadership? Lawyers and spokespersons from both corporate and government entities are saying, "A leader's private behavior is immaterial to his exercise of leadership in the public arena. As long as a leader is able to skillfully accomplish the tasks required of the post and can produce positive results; it should not matter to anyone what belief that leader privately embraces or what behavior he or she engages in behind closed doors." In his book titled "Leading from the Inside – Out" (2000), Dr. Rima outlines several interesting points to help leaders to take inventory of their behaviors. He states, "personal character is defined as the integration of an individual's personal beliefs, value, and morals, which taken as a whole, reveal the true nature or character of that individual" (p.36). Judas Iscariot of the Bible comes to mind, and you almost feel sorry for a person like him. Why did he do it you might ask? CHARACTER! President Bill Clinton, when asked why he did it, he responded; "because I could," (Rima, 2000, p.37) CHARACTER again! Therefore, an individual's personal character will determine the path one takes. Therefore, in greatest business leadership, leaders must ask themselves several questions:

- Why must I have a good rapport with the congregation? (Social awareness)
It is essential because it will be difficult to get anything done without it. Members of your church will see more sense in you. This rapport will also instill trust, respect and belief toward you. They will be more subject to listen and believe you, more open-minded, more attentive and stable. With a good rapport communications will go well.
- Why is it important to be able to demonstrate leadership ability? (Self management) Being able to allow people to see your leadership in action is what is required by God to potentially lead in the first place. If you can't convince people that you have it, then you can't convince them to follow you. A leader must show people which way to go, by those abilities. Just having the ability is not enough; you must demonstrate it to them.
- Why is it essential that a leader be available and accessible to the membership? (Relationship management) Leadership is just that, giving people some attention - people like attention, and they want it regularly. Leadership is a 24/7 thing. Most people need the preacher and the elders for

prayers, feelings and personal matters. The leader must demonstrate to people that you are there for them, and with them. As their leaders you must be there; ready and dependable.

- Why must a leader maintain his temper and anxieties? (Self management and relationship management) As a leader you must be humble to your calling, if you can't control yourself; then how can you control and influence others. A leader must realize that these two things are a direct reflection upon him in the eyes of those he serves. A leader must keep a clear head, in order to make decisions to lead the flock.
- How important is it that a leader maintains appearance and manners? (Self awareness and social awareness) Appearances are everything; as a leader people have you under close scrutiny, they need to have your respect. Appearance and manners means a lot to people; they feel you must give God your best even with your appearance. This is important because we are role models; it is important how we look and behave.
- How important is it for a leader to study or take courses in self improvement? (Self management) As leaders we must stay ahead of our followers and students. Being open-minded to studies improves oneself; sets high standards, and gives you more

knowledge. A leader must constantly find ways to improve oneself. Since there is no end to learning, a leader must learn more in order to past it on to the flock.

A well-defined leader is one who is internally aligned in what they say and do. It looks like this: Their thinking rules their emotions, they're a non-anxious presence, they have firm and appropriate boundaries, they have clarity of self and their own goals, they consider self when problems arise, they welcome conflict that is centered on mission, they know their own core values and live them out in actions. As you can see, it begins with learning about self, the good (core values) and what you struggle with anxieties (Manz & Neck, 2013). Leadership always begins with truly understanding who you are and what's important to you. It moves to what your weaknesses may be. Knowing the good and the gaps of you is the core to good leadership. You can always gain knowledge and learn new skills, but even before you do—learn about yourself. So, if you want to grow in your leadership, take the time to know yourself. This is essential to leading in the world's greatest business, the Church.

Chapter 11

Questions for Reflection and Discussion

1. Why do some leaders reach the point of feeling that they have certain entitlements?

2. In your own words, explain the significance of self-leadership.

3. Explain how you balance home, work, and church and community life.

4. What is the significance of establishing a rapport with your membership or team members?

5. As a leader, how do your address or handle harmful temptation?

Chapter 12
Modeling Leadership (Team Building)

"If you want to lead, you must be among them"

Now, let's have a talk about team building or empowering others. At first glance, it does appear to be incongruous, and that is because of the "every man for himself" philosophy, which is wide-spread in our society. Conversely, every man is to first effectively develop and govern self and his own family, a small society, before he governs a larger one, the Church (1Timothy 3:4, 5; 4:10-16). Someone said, that the "home is the boot camp for church leadership". But even at that, the family is a team too. J. Paul Getty once said, "I would rather have 1% of one hundred other's efforts than 100% of my own efforts working for me." He was willing to share his substance with others, in return for greater profits. A leader must be willing to share his knowledge and experience with the team. There first must be self-leadership, before there can be team/group leadership. This means that the leader must develop him or herself to their highest potential, but must also be willing to share his time, his space and his substance. The apostle Paul tells Timothy, that the things I have taught you, to past them on to others. As I have empowered you, you must in return empower others (2Timothy 2:2).

Not a One Man Show!

In recent years, organizations and researchers have come up with the concept of Shared Leadership as an innovative approach to team building. Shared leadership, according to Pearce and Conger (2003) is the shifting of leadership responsibilities to others in the group or organization within the environment that the group operates. Everyone is responsible for leadership in the organization. If bad behavior is noticed everyone is held accountable. It promotes and participates in the purpose of the organization more so than the mission of the organization. Although the concept was originally proposed many decades ago, Pearce and Conger (2003) define shared leadership as "a dynamic, interactive influence process among individuals in groups for which the objective is to lead one another to the achievement of group or organizational goals" (p.1). According to numerous scholars addressing shared leadership, there are several common commonalities in their explanation of what constitutes or defines the theory; in that, it increases innovativeness, empowers individuals and demands accountability for members contributing toward the common mission (Wassenaar & Pearce, 2012). One of the strengths of shared leadership is that it promotes teamwork, consideration of others and unity. Furthermore, Participative leadership theories suggest that the ideal leadership style is one that takes the input of others into account. These leaders encourage participation and contribution from group members and help group members feel more relevant and committed to the decision-making process. In this, the leader retains the right to allow the input of others. Supportive leadership is a kind of leadership, where you listen to your subordinates and help them out when they need help. Supportive leadership helps to build and maintain effective interpersonal relationships. Even though all of this sounds good, we need to be reminded that the Apostle Paul first echoed these expressions:

….."[11] "But all these worketh that one and the selfsame Spirit, dividing to every man severally as he will……..[18] But now hath God set the members every one of them in the body, as it hath pleased him.[19] And if they were all one member, where were the body? [20] But now are they many members, yet but one body. [21] And the eye cannot say unto the hand, I have no need of thee: nor again the head to the feet, I have no need of you.[22] Nay, much more those members of the body, which seem to be more feeble, are necessary……That there should be no schism in the body; but that the members should have the same care one for another……whether one member suffer, all the members suffer with it; or one member be honored, all the members rejoice with it. ²⁷ Now ye are the body of Christ, and members in particular" (NKJV).

Moses needed help too!

Furthermore, it was a firsthand experience that reminds me of when I first came into the Kingdom, I was a serious evangelistic worker, but I found myself doing more and more shepherd type work, fixing things. Even though shepherding is kingdom work, I felt kept from one-on-one ministry. I felt like I could do more for the Kingdom with individual effort, than working with others. Fortunately, I learned that even though that my heart was in the "field", my labors and skills were more so needed in the "laboratory"; that is, working with and developing others (2 Timothy 2:2). Jesus said, "that he who is great among you, he must be the servant of all (Matthew 23:11). Therefore, we should not be afraid to plan spiritual work with others. Many New Testament Believers were active in evangelism and service (Acts 8:4). In the book of Acts, we witness an evangelistic zeal and endeavor to bring the community outside the church to salvation in Jesus Christ (Acts 2:47). In short, this is called team building in the world's greatest business, the Church. My experiences with the shared leadership concept have been prevalent in the ministry context. For instance, there is an inherent division of labor for the elders and for the evangelist/minister of the local church (Acts 20:28; 2Timothy 4:1-6). Each has different functions but the same goal or objective is to support the spread of the gospel and to strengthen the body (Ephesians 4:11-16). Therefore, if you serve in the church in any capacity consider it an honor to lead in the world's greatest business, the Church.

Chapter 12
Questions for Reflection and Discussion

1. What does it mean as a family man to put God first in your life?

2. How do you relate being a supportive leader to being a father?

3. Explain how 1 Corinthians 12:11-17 helps you to lead and avoid the need to be in the spot-light.

4. In your own words, how does Participative leadership theory make you a great leader?

5. Explain how you would lead one of your team members who is more qualified to do what the team does than you are.

Chapter 13
Modeling Leadership (Organizational)

"If you want to lead, you must speak their language"

And finally, we have come to where we examine the overall strength of our leadership from an organizational perspective. The significance of organizational leadership is that the culture of the organization is determined by its model and the effectiveness of its leaders (Shein, 2010). Sense organizations grow and age with time, change will take place. Organizational leadership is challenged with great responsibilities such as ensuring sustainability, growth, and development. Leaders make a meaningful difference in every aspect of organizations. We want and expect leadership that is purposeful and intelligent, effective and competent, and caring and moral (Conger, 2016). The big concern then would be, in order to have healthy organizations you must have healthy leadership. Certainly, this is in line with Apostle Paul's admonition to the Ephesians Elders "take heed to yourselves and to all the flock, over which the Holy Ghost has made you overseers to feed the Church of God which he has purchased with his own blood" (Acts 20:28). Subsequently, church leadership is faced with the same challenges as leaders in secular contexts; as the church has a concern with unity and growth, even in the mist of handling conflict. Ironically, there is the realization that there are many institutions in the world that are making progress and meeting their goals, and are doing a great good for mankind. However, there is only one that is truly concerned with the affairs of Christ; this institution is the Church, which is expected to promote His cause on earth. It is very important that those who consider themselves as God's children understand what it really involves in growing his church.

At the opening chapters of this book there was a discussion of whether the church is to be viewed as a business, and whatever your view might be at this point, there are biblical principles and some secular concepts that will cause the church to grow. I believe that we must view the church not only as church community, but also as a corporation and as a cause. The church in metaphorical terms is viewed or described in scripture as a community or as a family (Acts 2:42-47; 4:32-36). The family has core valves – love, loyalty, and mutual support (1Cor. 12:24-26). We care for the weakest one among us and we treat them as brothers and sisters and mother and fathers (1Tim. 5:1-2). Even thou the churches core values consist of love, loyalty, and mutual support; there are times when we must reprove, rebuke with all longsuffering and doctrine (2 Timothy 4:2; Galatians 6:1-2). But also, the church is metaphorically described as an institution, corporation with officers and leaders (Phil. 1:1; Eph. 4:11-13). In (1 Corinthians 12: 8-11) is shown where the church is to manage itself, effectively and efficiently. In many ways the church is a business, in that, it is in the business of saving souls. Therefore, we must have an understanding of its mission, vision, its goals and standards (Luke 14:28-31). And again, the Bible also uses military metaphors – soldiers wear armor, war to be fought, those held captive by sin, need to be set free (Eph. 6:10-11). True soldiers don't really care about what color you are - just as long as we are fighting the same enemy for victory, survival, and a common cause (Eph. 4:8). The churches primary cause is to seek and save the lost, educate the world about Jesus Christ and present people anew in Christ Jesus (Eph. 3:9-11; Colossians 1:27).

The Twenty-Third Psalms

Fortunately, to the advantage of church leaders today, Franklin Camp in his book "Principles and Perils of Leadership" (1984) has truly blessed us leaders and students of leadership by presenting a lecture on the Twenty-third Psalms and applies it to shepherding-leadership. I have not replicated it in its entirety, but have presented the highlights of it, in my opinion. "The 23rd Psalms is considered the shepherd's psalm. It was written down to a shepherd, and it was written by a shepherd about a shepherd. This makes it even more interesting. It is a psalm of comfort, and it is appropriate at a funeral, but it has a much broader application. It was written for one who has been through the trials and the valley of the shadows of death but was still living. The psalm seems to have been written in the latter part of David's life, as he looked back over his past experience as a shepherd. The picture in this psalm is of God as a shepherd. Is this not an apt picture for Elders? Is it not their responsibility to provide guardians care and provisions for those who are under their oversight? The Lord is my shepherd; I shall not want. There are some things in this that are appropriate for shepherds of the flock to consider. While God was the shepherd of the flock, He was also David's personal shepherd. There are some things that are suggested by David in speaking of the Lord as his shepherd. God has a heart of a shepherd, indicating his love for the sheep. God sacrifices for the sheep, so the shepherd sacrifices for the sheep. God has the eyes of a shepherd, that is, He takes in all the flock and does not miss even one sheep that goes astray" (Camp, 1984).

The need still exists!

In today's society, it will take spiritual, transformational and servant leadership in the Lord church in order to remain the world's greatest business. Leadership with a spirit of humility and service will cause people to follow you because they want to, not because they have to. Transformational leaders motivate and inspire people by helping group members see the importance and higher good of the task (Bass, 2010). Certainly, within my church context, it will require transformational leadership in conveying to members that there are times one must adapt to the situation, even when it calls for a change in a person's normal way of operating or functioning. Moreover, it is my impression that my context would be appreciative of the potential results that can come from the implication of servant leadership which suggests that the leader's humility and teamwork spirit induces the follower to commit to the leader and his cause. This theory compliments my giftedness and experiences so that I am able to incorporate its tenants into my context, as it would contextually resonate with my church (Northouse, 2013). Leadership in the church is expected to unify the members, in order to evangelize the world (Ephesians 3:9-11).

United we stand, divided we fall (Ephesians 4)

When we speak of unity we are speaking of being involved with those who share common goals, interests, and ideals. The Apostle Paul encourages the Philippians to "stand fast in one spirit, with one mind striving together for the faith of the gospel" (Philippians 1:27). It must be understood that unity does not come easy; it takes a great effort to acquire it and a greater effort to maintain it. There is a risk of keeping unity. Question! What could happen in a church that would cause it to lose its unity? 1) Controversy amongst its members concerning true doctrine and teaching of error (Acts 15:1-20). 2). Conflicts between its leaders (Acts 15:36-41). 3) An oversight of potential problems (Acts 6:1-5). When these things occur leaders must identify or recognize them, correct them and move on beyond them. Question! What would be the challenge to keep the unity? Clearly define the mission of the church, (Ephesians 3:10-4:15); clearly define the role of each member, (Romans 12:4-9); develop everyone to their highest potential, (1 Corinthians 15:58) and motivate them to work together (Philippians 1:27).

Evangelism, is still the life blood of the Church
The organization and worship of the local church naturally focus attention on edification – the office of elders (pastors) speaks to the work of building up the saints, benevolence – the office of deacons along with weekly contribution speaks to supplying the needs of the saints. Unless frequent attention is given to Evangelism, it can become easy for churches to focus solely on edification and benevolence and to neglect evangelistic efforts both as congregations and as individuals. To neglect evangelism is harmful to the spiritual life of the church. Let's ask God to forgive us if we have been neglecting this important duty.

Evangelism goal setting makes some people nervous, but so does goal setting in other aspects of life. What I am suggesting is that we must so love God, so believe the Gospel, and so grieve over a lost world that we are willing to try whatever that works in carrying out the Great Commission. The growth of the early church was a direct consequence of the obedient co-laboring of the Christians. Believers were active in prayer, evangelism, and service. In the book of Acts, we see an evangelistic zeal and endeavor to bring the community outside the church to salvation in Jesus Christ. We have no excuse today to be ill-equipped, ill-informed, and unprepared in our outreach efforts (1 Corinthians 3:6-7). Is it possible for the church to experience real growth today? Yes! The Gospel of Christ is as powerful as ever (Romans 1:16). People are dissatisfied and are looking for a better way. God's power within us enables us to do more than we can imagine. (Eph. 3:20).

Therefore, as a church leader it is vitally important to have a panoramic view of your flock while you are actively circulating in its midst. Understanding organizational concepts both spiritual and secular will carry you a long way and sustain your flock. Therefore, if you serve in the church in any capacity consider it an honor to lead the world's greatest business, the Church.

Chapter 13
Questions for Reflection and Discussion

1. On a scale of 1 to 5, do you find yourself being more of a follower than a leader? Why? (1 being the lowest and 5 the highest)

2. In what way(s) have you notice that the church functions as a business?

3. Explain how the 23rd Psalms encourages and promotes church leadership

4. What is the significance of maintaining unity in your church or organization?

5. Explain best practices for Christians to best handle church conflict

An Open Discussion

At the onset of this book, I presented a two-fold purpose. First, to encourage Christian leadership and education, by conveying and emphasizing what is required of those who would find themselves leading in the world's greatest business, the Church. And second, to make aware the recognition of Church Leadership Education and Experience (CLEE), as an appropriate fit to corporate or secular academic success which is often presented with bias and prejudice that suggest that (CLEE) is not usually considered viable in the marketplace. Thus, presenting the case that (CLEE) embodies modern leadership theories, and is equal to or greater than secular education and corporate leadership instruction.

So, perhaps the question still remains, just what are they (secular disciplines) looking for or what is it that they don't want as they make their institutions, organizations, and businesses successful? As proposed by Camp (1984), "The greatest business in the world has to be the most far-reaching, most numerical in terms of employees and more financially stable than any other business in the world, most would agree" (p. 23). Personally, I think it's a fair and relevant criterion to measure worldwide success. In addition, I want to propose several questions for consideration that may be major factors as to determining the quality, viability, and effectiveness of pastoral or church leadership development in the marketplace.

- How does pastoral leadership roles in local churches, produce leaders that impact local, state and regional economies?
- What is the financial impact that churches have on the U.S. Economy?
- What is the level of influence that the Faith community and religious beliefs have on Politics?
- What is the role of Christian Educational Institutions in Improving Economic Self-reliance?
- What is the effectiveness of Ministerial leadership in local churches in comparison to that of chief executives of other local nonprofit organizations?

Perhaps if we had the answers to these above questions, a better understanding of why the church or pastoral leadership education and development and experience is met with bias and prejudice that suggests that it's usually not considered viable in the marketplace. And of course, we would have the answer to why church leadership education and experience should be highly considered as a viable resource in the marketplace wherever it may be.

Conclusion

The relativity of leadership theories as they apply to the leadership of churchmen:

According to the readings, there are several leadership theories that are comparable, and in many cases unique to the nature and the work of Ministry. Thus, by leading as an Elder, Bishop, Shepherd, Pastor, and Overseer one embodies shared, supportive, servant, spiritual and situational leadership. As a Deacon, one embodies servant, supportive and spiritual leadership. As a Preacher and an Evangelist one embodies transformational, servant, spiritual, situational and charismatic leadership. As a Teacher one embodies servant, supportive, spiritual and transformational leadership. As a Ministry Leader, one embodies servant and transformational leadership. And as Women in Church Leadership one embodies servant, transformatioinal, and supportive leadership. As with all church leaders, each has a bit of everything. It is my impression that these leadership theories will benefit the Eldership/ leadership of the church if developed and implemented.

According to Smith, Peterson, & Schwartz (2002), the culture of an organization is determined by the behavior of the leader(s) and in some instances, a leaders' behavior is shaped by the culture of the organization. Someone has said that an effective leader must be able to "Dream it up, Present it clearly, and get others in on it" (Winkler, 2003). Yes, as to Visionary Skills: leadership requires one to have an imagination, in order to form a vision and strategies for the organization. This is a part of one's conceptual skills allows a leader to be able to see the organization as a whole. Yes, as to Communication Skills: leaders have to be able to communicate effectively with all levels of the organization and even people outside the organization. Communication includes being able to ask questions and provide feedback, listen to others, being able to interpret body language. Without this skill, there is not any leading because people might not understand and therefore don't follow or they do not respect one because they misinterpret what is being communicated. Yes, as to Motivational Skills: a leader has to have the ability to sell their thoughts, vision, and strategies to everyone. If one cannot get people on board then they will not follow.

Without being able to create followers a leader does not exist. Great then, because Preachers' casts visions effectively and persuasively communicate and motivate daily year-in and year-out. My point is this, if these are the requirements to getting hired, considering all other credentials are in place; then what is the issue with having a Faith-based leadership background? Leaders in the early church such as overseers and deacons, had to meet a rigorous standard to be elected (1Timothy 3:1-78-13). Even Jesus, before he chose his twelve disciples, spent an entire night in prayer making sure he selected those his Father was giving him (Luke 6:12; John 17:6). These men were ordinary businesspeople, but their character allowed them to be fashioned into extraordinary apostles.

Moreover, it is my impression that churches, and all other secular and corporate entities would be appreciative of the potential results that can come from the implications of transformational and charismatic theories (House, 2010 and Bass, 2010). Also, the skills approach theory does complement the leadership style of churchmen (Kotter, 2010). Furthermore, the servant leader theory which suggests that the leader's humility and teamwork spirit induces the follower to commit to the leader and his cause, this theory too does resonate with church leadership (Northouse, 2013). In consideration of all that has been said, I am convinced that principles of leadership of faith-based origin are viable in the marketplace.

Appendixes

Welcome to a smorgasbord of concepts and procedures (some original and some garnered) this author has implemented with success as he endeavor to lead in the world's greatest business, the Church.

Check My Leadership

A church can never be larger or greater than its **Leadership**; in fact, a churches success is determined by the effectiveness of its **Leadership.**

Situation Review: Do you lead a ministry? _____ Have you ever led a ministry?_____

Indicate how you agree with the following statements (2 = strongly agree; 1 = agree; 0 = disagree).

1. I have several strong personal needs I depend on my ministry team to satisfy_____.

2. I am a positive spiritual influence on the members of my ministry team_____.

3. I interact with my team members primarily on a professional level and not so much on a personal one _____.

4. I regularly pray with the members of my ministry team _____.

5. I rely on my formal authority (position power) to make things happen within the ministry _____.

6. I feel responsible for nurturing the growth of my team members spiritually as well as professionally _____.

7. I value my team members primarily for the contributions they make to the ministry _____.

8. The ministry team members often come to me for advice and counsel _____.

9. I spend about the same amount of time with each of my team members _____.

10. I have a strong sense of conviction that God is supporting me and the ministry work I do _____.

11. People don't always listen to what I have to say or follow my advice _____.

12. I view my work more as a ministry to serve God than as a profession that enable me to make a living _____.

Total your odd-numbered statements _____ (**poor leadership practices**) and then your even-numbered _____ (**positive leadership practices**) thus subtracting odd-numbered from your even-numbered. If the difference is below (5), you need to seek advice pertaining to leadership.

Family Meeting

February 8, 2015

Community + Corporation + Cause

Mission Statement

Our mission is to bring others to Christ through proclaiming the "Good News" that salvation has come to all men. Romans 1:16; Titus 2:10, 11; 1Timothy 2:4, 5

Meeting Purpose

Our time together as a family is to discuss where we are, where we are headed, and how we are going to get there. But what is most important, is that we all get involved.

Our immediate objectives as a family is to be of "one accord" and to strengthen our leadership; to provide a safe haven for everyone; to establish accountability, and provide tools and support to <u>move the church forward</u>.

Furthermore, as we move forward we will evaluate our current situation (the church's mindset), assess our membership, and examine our current ministries for revitalization or enhancement.

What have we done? (Recently)

- Acquired a fulltime Preacher/Evangelist
- Launched a new Sunday School curriculum

- Conducted a successful Youth Sunday (a first)
- Conducted a Men's Leadership meeting
- Conducted a Evangelistic Bible Study Training Class
- Initiated a Inviting Guest project
- Minister sent outreach letters to membership and parents of SCA students
- A church Family meeting scheduled and conducted
- Conducted a Membership Assessment Survey

Results of Survey
(What you said)

Your personal church-related needs of the church: I want to learn to teach others and teach our teens to teach; know more of the history of the local church; some teaching on tardiness; lessons on stress of this life; more knowledge of the Gospel; Bible study teaching techniques; more support and love from other ministries; teaching on the End of Times; more visually presented sermons; leadership to encourage the women more (publicly), and a greater commitment in support of them; enhance the learning of songs and training of our song leaders.

What you think should take place around here: more encouragement from Eldership, more helpers and more leaders and involvement from members; church needs to get involved in more mission work; need to have a "Ladies Day" program and work day for the Lord; a Gospel Concert and Spiritual Growth workshop, plus an Outreach effort to other churches of Christ in this region; new convert class and door knocking; do more things with teens; more parental involvement with teens; weekly night out for fellowship; in home bible study group; better relationship between school and the church; weekly VBS/L2L program; more activities for teens; more Christian family involvement; Gospel meeting-- revival, more structure, inner church involvement; more transparent leadership and trust and delegation and teamwork; more outreach in the community; more mentoring relationship between older and young adult sisters in the church.

Where are we headed?

- Respond to results of **Membership Survey (Bringing out the Best in Others).**
- Conduct follow-up meetings and training involving church leadership. An ongoing weekly to bi-weekly effort is in the works.

- Conduct follow-up training in **Evangelistic Bible Study** and conduct a second class for those who could not attend the first one.
- Conduct **Ministry Design** class on 2/22/15, from 4:30 – 6:45, designed to increase effectiveness and sustainability of ministry efforts.
- Initiate a **New Members Orientation Breakfast**. An assimilating endeavor for immediate involvement of new converts and new members.
- Conduct a **Membership Retention Awareness** workshop. An effort to keep the sheep in the fold.
- Conduct a **Women's Leadership Training** program
- Set and pursue a goal of adding **30 new families** to our number by year end; by consistently inviting 200+ guests each month.

QUESTIONS AND ANSWERS:

Creating a Successful Ministry

Ministry Leaders……… your time has come!

(1) Set Directions
- Vision
- Mission
- Shared Purpose
- Strategy

(2) Gather and Deploy Resources
- Articulate needs
- Make a case for Resources

(3) Assemble the Team
- Skills
- People
- Chemistry/trust

(4) Allocation of work and
- Balance workload across team
- Set attainable and realistic goals
- Prioritize

(5) Execute Plan
- Make decisions
- Measure results

(6) Motivate and Inspire team
- Empower team

- Give authority to do job
- Feedback
- Resolve conflicts

(7) Develop team long term
- Build depth- skills development
- Create assignments that stretch the team
- Allow for spiritual growth

Church Growth Workshop

The Key to Church Growth

Introduction: It is imperative that we understand that we exist for the express purpose of glorifying God through Christ and his church, as we seek and save the lost. We must proclaim the good news of the Gospel that salvation has come to all men and to reach with the Gospel as many as possible in the communities that surround us, and those who are a part of our lives in other communities.

Our vision must be to train, strengthen and heal families through the Gospel. To establish a system that will challenge and develop the church both spiritually and socially. To numerically increase the involvement of its members and to recapture the focus of those who are assembling by identifying their needs and abilities.

We must also be committed to bringing out the best in others in relation to God, one another, the world and oneself. We must believe that it's only as we receive more of the claims and teachings of Jesus the Christ, who is the way, the truth and the life that we will ever have anything to share with others.

We must forever remember that the message of the church is the basic need of the human life. Our time together is to discuss church growth is the context of where we are as a church, where are we headed and how important it is for us to get there.

But what is more important than the above mentioned is that all Christians need to be involved. We will discuss guidelines, ministry leadership, evangelistic and community outreach aspects of church growth.

Expectations of Church Growth

The Lord Jesus desires for his church to grow in two ways. He wants Christians to become more like himself by learning and practicing the teachings of the New Testament (Ephesians 4:14; 2 Peter 3:18) this is spiritual growth. He also desires others to become members of his church by being saved (Luke 19:10; John 3:16; 1Timothy 2:4) this is numerical growth.

The book of Acts records the amazing numerical growth of the church in the first century (Acts 2:41, 47; 4:4; 5:14; 6:7; 8:1-4). There were many that opposed Christianity, yet in spite of all the disadvantages and difficulties, the church grew rapidly and soon the Gospel had spread throughout the world! (Colossians 1:23). Since the Gospel of Christ is as powerful as ever (Romans 1:16); it is still possible for the church to have rapid growth now!

Many people are dissatisfied and are looking for a better way. God's power within us enables us to do more than we can imagine (Ephesians 3:20). The realization can be felt if we will:
- Exalt Jesus Christ
- Spend more time in prayer
- Love one another
- Be joyful
- Help every Christian feel important and appreciated
- Practice biblical teaching regarding leadership
- Have preaching and teaching that produce growth
- Concentrate on the mission of the church
- Be flexible in method and
- Have faith in God.

God's power working in us enables us to do much more than we are able to ask for in prayer or even imagine. Therefore, we should not be afraid to plan and undertake spiritual work that we feel unable to accomplish by our human efforts and resources.

Ministry Leadership - Romans 12:5-8
It is evident from scripture that there is something for every member of the church to do. However in every organization that is functional; it's only functional because someone is leading it. Therefore, the Lord's church must have members who will lead well. Christian leadership resides in the person more than the position. This principle is found throughout the scriptures.

Leaders in the Bible led because of their relationship with God, not because they were expert managers (Exodus 4:1-4). Christian leadership is a matter of personal spiritual maturity and growth. People are attracted to spiritually mature people and responsive to their influence. Those who God calls to ministry leadership, He first called them to spiritual maturity (Joshua 1:1-7; Numbers 13:31; Romans 16:1-2). Ministry leaders work more through influence (role modeling) than power (formal authority).

People follow them because they want to, not because they must (2 Timothy 2:2; Philippians 3:16-17). Church growth is generational, Paul instructed Timothy to teach other men that they will be able to teach others also (2 Timothy 1:4, 2:2). A church can never be larger or greater than its Leadership. In fact, a church's success is determined by the effectiveness of its Leadership (Hebrew 13:7).

Since Christ's model of leadership is based on sacrificial service to others, Christian leaders expect to serve rather than to be served. This requires that we subordinate our own needs and attend to the needs of others. Ministry leaders are able to build themselves into others because of the overflowing of their spiritual blessings. Those who have the most, serve the most (Luke 12:48).
Therefore, when those who are in leadership roles truly lead; the church will then grow.

Evangelism – Matthews 28:18-19
Mankind from the beginning was created to glorify God, but man failed. It repented God to have made the man; nevertheless, God designed the plan of redemption because of his love, his wisdom and executed it by his power. God is just as interested in the salvation of mankind today as he was thousands of years ago (Romans 1:16; 1Timothy 2:4). The early Christians were characterized by zeal and fervor that cause them to go "house to house." The work of converting souls to Christ and making disciples was done by individuals; communicating their faith to those who needed to be saved. Let it forever be upon our minds as we study the importance of this subject (2 Corinthians 4:7).

Evangelism: the process of bringing one that is lost to a saved condition in Christ through the

Gospel. It is what takes place when those who were lost, change their allegiance to Christ and become converts. It is presenting Christ, lifting him up, exposing people to him. We must let men see His person, His plan and bring them into an atmosphere or place of decision where Christ's drawing power can affect a life. It is the activity or act of spreading the Good News of the Gospel in a particular area, in a particular way, at a particular time and for a particular reason.

Evangelism is the responsibility of the church; the church is the fulfillment of God's eternal purpose. The church is the consummation of his plan on earth; it is to make known God's wisdom; in which God is glorified (Ephesians 1:20-23; 5:23-27; 3:9-11, 21).

Evangelism is a mandate of God. When we consider this mandate we must consider at least four aspects of it. We must understand that it is a commission; the act of committing, doing, the act of trust, a trust, a charge, a certificate which confers a particular authority (Matthews 28:18, 19; Mark 16:15, 16). It's a concept; thus lifting up Christ by going after wasted lives and presenting them anew in Christ (John 12:32; 20:21; Galatians 2:20). Its compassion; having pity for someone in distress and doing what it takes to deliver them from their misery (John 5:1-8).

And there is the continuity of it; being willing to maintain a good work, thus keeping the task alive (Titus 2:14; 3:1, 8, 14). When the time comes to share the word of the Gospel; most of us are known to panic. We know the world's most life-changing secret, and when it's time to tell it, we choke. We must understand that we are the vessels that God uses to bring fallen man back to Him. God is holding us responsible, let's not disappoint Him.

Community Outreach – Acts 2:41-47
It must be forever remembered that the growth of the early church was a direct consequence of the obedient co-laboring of the Christians. Believers were active in prayer, evangelism, and service. In the book of Acts, we can see an evangelistic zeal and endeavor to bring the community outside of the church, to salvation in Jesus Christ. We have no excuse today to be ill-equipped, ill-informed and unprepared in our outreach efforts.

There are some questions that we must first ask ourselves when we consider community outreach.

- Do we have a necessary presence in the community? John 10:8

- Why do we exist? That is, what needs in the community would not be meet if our church were not around (Luke 4:18).

- Why do people come to our church rather than to others? (Acts 19:23-24).

- To what kind of people and groups are we best prepared to minister unto (Acts 10:14, 28)?

There is some spiritual advice that we must receive:

- Numbers are valued because people are valued (1Timothy 2:4).

- Kingdom advancement is the results of sacrifice (Acts 2:44, 45).

- A sign of maturity is not tenure, but rather service and reproduction (Matthews 11:28; 28:19).

- Good deeds will produce openness to Good Gospel (Acts 2:47).

Do we really understand what really happened on the cross?

Do we know the good news of the cross and how we can take the advantage of it (Matthews 25:35-40)?

Do we understand that God made man good and that man turned bad and has been trying to find his way back to God, but has been doing it in the wrong way, man's way (Proverbs 14:12; 16:25)?

Thus not accepting the fact that the only way back to God is through Jesus Christ the Son (John 14:6).

IF YOU WANT TO EVANGELIZE

Every Christian has the fundamentals necessary to become a successful winner of souls. However, in order to become one, certain attitudes must be developed, personalities cultivated, and specific preparations must be made. So then, how can we regain lost ground and become friends of Publicans and Sinners just as Jesus did?

- We must overcome our "Holier than thou" attitudes—Luke 18:14
- We must learn to live the Christian life on the offensive as well as the defensive if we want to draw close to sinners. James 1:27
- We must be physically present with Publicans and sinner if we want to be their friend Like 15: 1
- To become friends to sinners, we must become likable people. "They don't like grouches and those whose noses are in the air", Luke 2:52, Acts 2:47
- We must learn to turn friendship into evangelistic opportunities if we want to be genuine friends of sinners. John 4
- We must be quick to appreciate and slow to criticize Luke 19:10

- We must resist the temptation to pre-judge the "Receptivity" of sinners. Acts 9:13
- Do I consider this visit an actual spiritual service, or is it merely a social call?
- Is it my primary purpose to win a soul to Christ, or win an argument?
- Are my habits ones about which I will have to apologize?
- Do I look upon this work as a privilege of sharing my life with Christ, or as a boring task which I have been begged into doing?
- Have a genuine love for humanity; **(Smile)** let the world know that you are happy.
- Make the people crave for what you have, make the Gospel attractive.
- We must be **convinced** that God is always with us to help us and **that His word is powerful.**

"We have the greatest message this world has ever known, Millions are searching for it. Since they have not all found it, they have accepted the philosophy of men, and this worldly system. They would gladly give-up those things for the pure Gospel, if they only knew and were persuaded to believe, trust and obey".

Benjamin A. Griffin

CHURCH CONSULTING

What is church consulting?
Church consultation begins with a clear goal of analyzing existing conditions in a church and suggesting improvements for its overall health. It is a process where a qualified consultant, who is not a member of the organization provides insights and recommendations to improve how well the church functions according to the purposes of the church, as described in Acts 2:42-47.

I've heard of church growth. What does church health mean?
The idea of church growth is often related to numbers – the number of new members, persons baptized into the church, etc. Church health is related to how well the body of Christ functions in terms of fulfilling God's mission and purpose. Healthy churches are most effective when the six purposes of Acts 2:42-47 are <u>intentional</u>, <u>active</u> and <u>balanced</u>:

- Fellowship
- Worship
- Ministry
- Discipleship
- Evangelism
- Prayer

What do church consultants do?
Based on the goals of the church, consultants perform one or more of the following services when called on by the church leaders:

- Listen
- Investigate
- Recommend
- Encourage change
- Analyze
- Help implement change, when needed

What areas are covered in a comprehensive consultation?
Church consultations vary in terms of their focus and intensity. Most focus on specific areas of church health. This consultation focuses on the following areas:

1. Planning/goal setting
2. Growth barriers
3. Outreach/evangelistic approaches
4. Mission/vision
5. Assimilation effectiveness
6. Communication effectiveness
7. Worship issues
8. Leadership effectiveness
9. Personnel issues
10. Ministry staff alignment

What are the steps involved in a church consultation?

Church consultation services may vary widely, though the most effective consultants include each of the following steps in their work (in sequential order):

1. Consultation request
2. Initial interview
3. Proposal to church leadership
4. Acceptance
5. Consultation work
6. Initial verbal report to leadership
7. Written report (presented to leadership)
8. If needed, proposal for future action
9. Follow-up

What consultation approach is most effective?

There are varying approaches which have various results; however, Plumline Leadership has adopted the collaborative consulting role.

In a collaborative consulting situation:

- The consultant and the church work to become interdependent.
- Decision making is characterized by mutual exchange and respect for the responsibilities and expertise of both the consultant and the church community.
- Data collection and analysis are joint efforts.
- Collaboration is considered essential.

- Communication is two-way.
- Implementation and responsibilities are determined by discussion and agreement.
- The consultant's goal is to allow the church community to gain abilities for the future.
- Ownership of the results is most likely to be claimed by the church.

About the Author

Ben Griffin is the founder, and the President of Plumline Leadership LLC. He is currently pursuing an Ed.D in Organizational Leadership-Conflict Resolution and he holds a D. Min. in Leadership and Organizational Development, a MAM in Leadership Studies, MPA certificate in Strategic Management, a Masters and Bachelors in Ministry, and is a School of Preaching Graduate.

He's a native of Pensacola, Florida. He's married with five adult children, six grandchildren. He presently preaches in Lake Worth, Florida. Following his Army discharge in 1985, he enrolled at Bellview Preaching Training School, and over the past thirty-six years he has preached the Gospel in every southeastern state, including Texas and has preached full-time for churches in Florida, Alabama, and North & South Carolina.

He has assisted many churches in leadership development. He composes leadership and outreach training materials. He served nine years in the U.S. Army as a Staff Sergeant. He participates in community leadership projects, serves as a board president for Suncoast Christian Academy, is a member of Society for Church Consulting, Association for Talent Development and provides mentoring for "at risk" kids.

"Without effective Leadership that's constantly developing; Evangelism that consistently presents people anew in Christ; and a church that comforts its hurting and strengthens its weak......nothing else about church really matters"

-Benjamin A. Griffin

www.plumlineleadership.com

Bibliography / References

Anderson, Lynn (1997). *They Smell like Sheep*, Spiritual Leadership for the 21st Century, Howard Publishing, West Monroe, La

Bass, Bernard M., (2010). *From Transactional to Transformational Leadership, Learning to Share the Vision* (pp. 256-260), In Leadership Classics, J. Timothy McMahon, (Ed), Waveland Press Inc., Longrove, Illinois

Blackaby, H. & Blackably, R. (2011). *Spiritual leadership,* Moving people onto God's Agenda, *B*&H Publishing Group, Nashville, Tennessee

Bredfelt, Gary (2006). *Great Leaders - Great Teachers*, Recovering the Biblical Vision for Leadership, Moody Press

Camp, Franklin (1987). *Principles & Perils of Leadership*, Camp Publications. Birmingham, Ala

Chen, C., & Yang, C. (2012). *The Impact of Spiritual Leadership on Organizational Citizenship Behavior*: A multisampling analysis. Journal of Business Ethics, 105(1), 107-114. doi:10.1007/s10551-011-0953-3

Cole, Edwin Louis (1982). *Maximized Manhood*, A Guide to Family Survival Whitaker House, New Kensington, Pa

Conger, J. A., (2016). *Charismatic Leadership, In G.R. Hickman (Ed.),* Leading organizations: Perspectives for a new era (pp. 56-60). Thousand Oaks, CA: Sage

Farrar, Steve (1990). *Point Man*, How A Man Can Lead His Family, Multnomah Publishers, Sisters, Oregon

Ferguson, Everett (2001). *Women in the Assembly*, Institute for Church and Family, Harding University Lectures

Getz, Gene A. (2003). *Elders and Leaders*, God's Plan for leading the Church; A Biblical, Historical, and Cultural Perspective, Moody Publishers, Chicago

Greenleaf, R K., (2016). *Servant Leadership*, In G.R. Hickman (Ed.), Leading organizations: Perspectives for a new era (pp. 56-60). Thousand Oaks, CA: Sage Publication

Fry, L. W. (2003). *Toward a Theory of Spiritual Leadership*. The Leadership Quarterly, 14(6), 693-727.

House, Robert J., (2010). *Path-Goal Theory of Leadership*, (pp. 313-315), In Leadership Classics, J. Timothy McMahon, (Ed), Waveland Press Inc., Longrove, Illinois

Johnson, Aubrey (2014). *Dynamic Deacons*, Champions of Christ's Church, Aubrey Johnson Ministries, Sharpsburg, Ga

Kaya, A., (2015). *The Relationship between Spiritual Leadership and Organizational Citizenship Behaviors*: A Research on School Principals' Behaviors Educational Sciences: Theory & Practice • 2015 June • 15(3) • 597-606 Department of Education Management and Inspection, Harran University, Şanlıurfa Turkey

Kotter, John (1996). *Leading Change*, Harvard Business Review Press

Malphurs, A. & Mancini, W. (2004). Building Leaders, Blueprint for Developing Leaderhip at Every level of your Church, Baker Books, Grand Rapids

Manz, C., & Neck, C. (2013). *Mastering Self-leadership:* Empowering yourself for personal excellence *(6th ed.).* (pp. 129-137). Abilene, Texas

Marquardt, M. J. (2011). *Building the Learning Organization* (2nd ed.). Boston: Nicholas Brealey.

Chps 1and 2. Excellence, (pp. 1-13), *6th ed. Upper Saddle River, NJ: Pearson Education, Inc.*

Mills, D. Quinn (2005). *Leadership,* How to Lead, How to Live.

Myers, J.B. (2003). *Elders and Deacons,* A Biblical Study of Church Leadership, pp 191-193, 21st Century Christian Publishing, Nashville, Tennessee

Northouse, Peter G., (2013). *Leadership:* Theory and Practice *(pp. 23,147,186-190)*, Sixth Edition, Sage Publication Inc, Thousand Oaks, California

Nye, Joseph, S. Jr., (2010). *Power and Leadership,* (pp.305-310), In Handbook of Leadership Theory and Practice, A Harvard Business School Centennial Colloquium, Harvard Business Review Press

Rima, D. Samuel (2000). *Leading from the Inside Out*, The Art of Self-Leadership, Baker Books, Grand Rapids, Mich.

Sanders, Oswald (2007). *Spiritual Leadership*, Principles of Excellence for Every Believer, 2007- Moody Publishers Chicago

Schein, Edgar H. (2010). *Organizational Culture and Leadership*, Jossey-Bass, A Wiley Imprint

Silvoso, Ed (2006). *Anointed for Business*, How to use your influence in the Marketplace to change the World, Regal Books

Smith, P. B., Peterson, M. F., & Schwartz, S.H. (2010). *Leadership and Cultural Context,* (pp.335-339), In Handbook of Leadership Theory and Practice, A Harvard Business School Publication

Strauch, Alexander (1995). Biblical Eldership, An Urgent Call to restore Bibleical Church Leadership, (pp. 122-123).

Wasserman, & Pearce (2012). In G.R. Hickman (Ed., *Leading Organizations*: Perspectives for a New Era. Thousand Oaks, CA: Sage Publication

Winkler, Wendell (2003). *Leadership:* The Crisis of Our Time, Winklers Publications

Yuki, G. (2010). *Management Dynamics in the Knowledge Economy*; Bucharest 2.1 (2014): 155-179

Made in the USA
Columbia, SC
04 January 2020